A HISTORY OF
ARCHITECTURE IN FRANCE

Frontis. The Panthéon, Paris (1757): a great Neo-Classical church by Soufflot. Its richly detailed Roman Corinthian interior is monumental but with the added elegance of the later eighteenth century. It shows the renewed preference at this time for the column rather than the pier.

A History of
ARCHITECTURE
in France

T. W. WEST M. A.

UNIVERSITY OF LONDON PRESS LTD

CONTENTS

LIST OF LINE DRAWINGS

LIST OF PLATES

ACKNOWLEDGEMENTS

The author and publishers thank the following for permission to reproduce photographs: F. A. Mella (plates 1a, 1b, 3, 5, 5b, 9, 10a, 11, 13, 14a, Foto Marburg; plate 5a; plates, 7, 8a, 14b, Foto Mairani; plate 12a, Phototèque Française; plate 15a, Archives Photographiques). The Mansell Collection (plates 6, 12b, 15b). Paul Popper Ltd (plates 2a, 2b, 10b, 16a). French Government Tourist Office (frontispiece, plate 8b). J. Allan Cash (plate 16b).

Grateful thanks are due to my wife for critical advice and encouragement, and to Mrs Ida Baker for her excellent work on the typescript of this and other books in the series.

T.W.W.

To Nicolas
who knows a good building
when he sees one

PREFACE

FOR well over a hundred years now Paris has been the chief centre of the art world, so that even foreign artists have had to win her favour and approval in order to receive international recognition and fame. In this respect, as in others, Paris is France, despite the rich diversity of her provinces.

The prestige of France in intellectual and artistic matters has always stood high, especially since the days of René Descartes, founder of modern philosophy and developer of scientific method, and of Louis XIV, *le Roi Soleil*. Then the artistic taste and manners of Versailles were eagerly followed even in those countries which in politics were firm enough to resist the expansionist ambitions of seventeenth-century France. Names like Racine in drama and Claude Lorrain in painting echoed across Europe and were not solitary expressions of the French genius or of France's 'invisible exports' in the economy of Western civilization.

The eighteenth century confirmed her high status, partly no doubt because she had by then become the largest, richest, and most powerful country on the Continent, but mainly by reason of the special distinction with which her intellectual and cultural achievements continued to grace her, among them the international reputations of Voltaire and the *philosophes*, Rococo and the art of Watteau, and the superb products of the factories of Gobelins and Sèvres with their tapestries and porcelain.

Classical French, that lucid, precise and elegant instrument of ideas was fostered by the Académie Française, founded by Cardinal Richelieu in the seventeenth century, and became the common language of educated Europe, the modern successor to the old unifying Latin tongue which had made Europe conscious of her shared heritage since the days of the Roman Empire. It is worth remembering, too, that the Latin contribution to the old Frankish language has its architectural counterpart in the classical relics of Provence, the most Latinized region of the old Roman province of Gaul.

Even when the *ancien régime* foundered in the high hopes, blood and violence of the Revolution and a new and better-ordered France emerged – to the dismay of her reactionary neighbours who would have preferred to stifle her – reform did nothing to abate her old cultural prestige to which were now added the resounding names of Napoleon's military successes in all their glittering panoply. Her writers and thinkers like the Encyclopédists, Montesquieu, and Rousseau were still avidly read and debated, while the classical motifs of the Empire style were as internationally fashionable as those of Louis Quinze had been. Later in the nineteenth century her philosophers and defenders of liberty, albeit chiefly in opposition, sustained her traditional role as the mother of enlightenment, while her creative energies found outlets in artists as diverse as Delacroix and Courbet in painting, Balzac and Flaubert in literature, and Berlioz and Debussy in music. Realism, Naturalism, and Impressionism were all reactions against the Romantic spirit of the earlier decades, breaking new ground and instinctively seeking a synthesis of Art and Science, still one of the great unresolved problems of our time.

The internationally minded aristocracy of eighteenth-century Europe had spoken French; now the new bourgeoisie were to follow. Of modern languages French was that principally adopted by English education in the nineteenth century, as much for the old reasons of intellectual training and cultural kudos as for social convenience and commercial interchange. With Cobden's Treaty of 1860, the traditional enemy across the narrow seas was becoming gradually transformed into the future trusted ally of *l'entente cordiale* and, on a more frivolous plane, the source of *haute couture*.

So much is to reflect, momentarily, a few of the gleaming facets of French culture generally; but to mention French architecture in particular is, for the majority of people, to conjure up equally few fleeting images: graceful medieval cathedrals soaring above the huddled roofs of old towns in the gentle Île de France, Picardy, and the valleys of Champagne; the romantic châteaux of Normandy and the garden of Touraine; the majestic palaces of the Louvre and Versailles; the grey and vaguely classical background of a great French city like Paris or Lyon and the whitewashed walls and low-pitched red pantiled roofs of the vernacular of the Mediterranean littoral at the other end of N.7.

In a way this is understandable. It is well-known that Gothic, or 'the French style' as it was known to its contemporaries, originated in France and was brought there during its earliest and freshest period to a peak of transparent logic and beauty. In the thirteenth century during the reign of Saint Louis Paris became the architectural pace-setter of Europe, and without being guilty of romanticizing the Middle Ages it is impossible not to see the great time-worn cathedrals as full of transcendent symbolic meaning and among the finest products of western civilization.

But to leave matters thus is to ignore an equally admirable achievement in classical architecture reaching from the sixteenth to the early nineteenth century. By this is meant no mere reproduction of imported Italian modes but a thoroughly Frenchified style as rational, sober, and elegant as the language of the academic tradition, with the subtlety of Molière and the polish of Lully. *Raison* and *clarté* are qualities to be found both in the Gothic and in the classical architecture of France. There was also the inventive fantasy of Rococo to complement the stricter classicism, as Fragonard's *fêtes galantes* are in a different world from Poussin.

True, French classicism could be pompous and occasionally dull, but at its best it was to produce some of the purest and most valuable gems in the crown of European architecture. The Early Renaissance châteaux of Chambord and Chenonceaux had not broken completely free of Gothic despite their innovations, but at Château de Maisons the full national Classicism emerges: all three are masterpieces of domestic building. In the noble domed churches of the Invalides and the Panthéon are examples of classical ecclesiastical architecture that are worthy to stand besides the great Romanesque churches of Aquitaine and Burgundy and even the Gothic glories of the cathedrals of Chartres, Reims, and Paris.

The tragedies which have befallen Europe in the last hundred years have brought home to many the emptiness and waste which follows in the wake of aggressive nationalism and the pursuit of *la gloire*, once so seductive to Frenchmen. The advances in law, administration and education, and the opportunity implied by the idea of *la carrière ouverte aux talents* of the First Empire were long remembered; the suffering it caused soon faded from memory. But the present generation, energetically committed to the forging of a new society founded on the application of science and the economic boom of the 1950's when France, primed by massive American aid, began once more to direct her own affairs with confidence and purpose, no longer regards the old ideals with the same nostalgia.

Yet for centuries, and especially since the First Republic, there has been throughout France a proud consciousness of a rich and unified national culture shared by all Frenchmen, from the north or from the Midi, whatever their regional loyalties, whatever their differences, physical and temperamental. Today there is no desire that this should be otherwise, only that the damaging aspects of Napoleonism should be replaced by a recognition of French power based on her growing industrial strength in the Community of Europe, and by a pre-eminence in thought and art of long continuity.

The last must embrace a respect for her great works of architecture inherited from the past. But in the nineteenth century the broad river of traditional French culture received, as a result of the genius of her inventors and the industrialization of the north which added new coal and metallurgical industries, a fresh and vitalizing tributary of intermingled technological and scientific currents, which in this century have taken over the main channel.

France has produced more than her share of scientists, engineers, and inventors. The famous École Polytechnique founded in 1794 was the first of its kind in the world. In building technology the 'engineering' materials of iron, steel, and above all reinforced concrete – a mainly French invention – were early adopted and energetically developed by engineers like Eiffel, Perret, and Freyssinet (the engineering element has always been important in French architecture), so that by the twentieth century the revolution of modern architecture was already under way, despite the profound conservatism of the École des Beaux-Arts and its academic tradition.

The ground was thus prepared for the seeds of Le Corbusier's genius which has flowered so prodigally and has been cross-fertilized with the forms and techniques of other pioneers who have worked outside France. Le Corbusier's influence is much less apparent in France than one would wish, but new and stimulating buildings are being created in ever greater numbers.

Since the Second World War change has become increasingly the order of the day, providing a more favourable atmosphere for public acceptance of modern architecture. Even the ultra-conservative French agriculture is changing and new sources of power have accrued to France like the immense quantities of natural gas in the Pyrenean foothills and the inexhaustible waters of the River Rhône. Great enterprises have sprung up whose physical embodiments are the new town and vast petro-chemical complex of Lacq, the magnificent hydro-electric dams of Donzère and Genissiat and the atomic power plant of Marcoule, near the ancient centre of Avignon. The latter has the tallest chimney in the world, while Tignes in the Val d'Isère has the highest dam, nearly 600 feet high.

We began by alluding to the enormous prestige of Paris in the arts of painting and sculpture. There is no comparable focus of world architecture, which today is many-centred; but it is more than evident that some of the most worthwhile work in contemporary architecture and urbanism is, after a notable delay, at last being created by French architects and planners. The Utopian idealism of Le Corbusier has provided launching pads for the future which are already being utilized by a generation which is destined to build more than has ever been built in the history of man. The great Unités d'Habitation of Marseille and Nantes, the new town of Marly-les-Grandes-Terres, near Paris, and structures as diverse as the new Gare de Montparnasse and recent churches like the Ronchamp chapel and Notre-Dame, Royan, are all fitting symbols of the resurgence of a great nation. The French contribution to the architecture of Europe is succinctly reviewed for the general reader (who, one hopes, is already attracted to the fair land of France and imbued with the spirit of the Concorde project) in the chapters which follow.

From about 1500 these are divided into centuries and the architecture does to some extent correspond to these chronological divisions. But it should be remembered that this is primarily a convenient device for arrangement and study; styles and movements do in fact overlap the centuries to a significant degree. To give but one example: the neo-classicism of the late eighteenth century runs without break into the First Empire, and even beyond, despite the virtual suspension of building activities in France between the Revolution and 1806.

In a survey as concise as this only those buildings which illustrate an evolutionary theme – particularly the first appearances of new forms and styles – or are outstanding in themselves, may be named, together with a handful of other representative examples from each period. It is impossible to refer to every work worth even the briefest mention; but sufficient indications, it is hoped, will be found to 'place' any building which the student or tourist may encounter on his travels.

There is no substitute for actual experience of buildings themselves. But as carefully conceived and created things they can never be entirely or satisfactorily assimilated as raw experience. Moreover, their age and complexity raise special barriers to direct experience. It is in these facts that the *raison d'être* of this short commentary chiefly lies.

'We are as dwarfs mounted on the shoulders of giants, so that although we perceive many more things than they, it is not because our vision is more piercing or our stature higher, but because we are carried and elevated higher thanks to their gigantic size.'

John of Salisbury, 12th-century English Bishop of Chartres, quoting the master of the episcopal school

'The purpose of construction is to make things hold together; of architecture to move us.'

Le Corbusier

CHAPTER ONE

The Earliest Centuries

PREHISTORIC

OF architecture proper in France there is nothing that dates from before the time of the Roman occupation of what was then Gaul. But of interest to all whose curiosity is roused by the habitations of man and his religious monuments are the many remains of prehistoric cultures which flourished there over periods far vaster than those which separate us from the fifth century, which saw the break up of the Roman Empire in the west. Chief among these perhaps are the cave dwellings of the Dordogne valley and the great stone monuments of Brittany.

La Cave, Padirac, Font de Gaume, and above all Lascaux show examples of the most primitive of all human shelters dating from Palaeolithic times, but as the paintings at Lascaux indicate from their location deep within the interior and away from the living spaces, they were also the centres of a magical art that was capable of depicting with astonishing naturalism the animals which were the source of life to those remote peoples. Thus the use of the caves by Cro-Magnon man some 20,000 years ago combines something of the home with something of the temple. Famous caves in the Pyrenees are the Mas d'Azil and Isturits which have also yielded the works of art of the earliest men.

Scattered over the north-west are many remains of the Neolithic peoples who succeeded the Ice Age, their impressive burial cairns, monoliths, and rudimentary stone structures consisting of two or three vertical stones carrying a horizontal member. These are called 'dolmens' or 'cromlechs' according to how many supporting uprights there are.

They are not confined to the north-west and may be found, for example, in Savoy, but Brittany is richest in such remains, Locmariaquer and Carnac being notable centres. At the latter there is a menhir or monolith over 60 ft high, the raising of which must have posed a considerable technological problem, like the erection of the trilithons at Stonehenge; but even more awe-inspiring are the *alignments* or long lines of stones arranged in avenues and focusing on the great stone altars.

The mysterious rituals associated with these vast dispositions will never be properly known, yet it cannot be doubted that here is one of the earliest examples of the human sense of spatial expression, one of the most fundamental elements of architecture. At Rodez there is a carved menhir.

So far structural development has been of the simplest kind, the placing of one stone across uprights. But this, too, is fundamental to architecture, the basis of all 'post and lintel' structures to come.

More interesting perhaps is the ancient system of corbelling where stones are laid in overlapping courses towards the centre of a structure, thus forming a primitive dome. The best early examples are those of Mycenae in Greece, but corbelling must have been a feature of certain kinds of later prehistoric stone buildings in France and it has survived almost unchanged, like the caelocanth, in the *borries* and well-covers of Provence or the strange sheep shelters of the Quercy district.

For the rest the history of prehistoric structures in France is much the same as in the other countries of Western Europe with Bronze Age 'hut circles' of stone and earth, roofed with timber and covered with turf or thatch of some sort. Gaul was the greatest centre of Celtic settlement, however, and the burial mound or great barrow near Châtillon-sur-Seine dating from *c.* 500 B.C. was a royal tomb and exceptionally impressive. Because of the presence of iron in those parts Minot in Burgundy also has remains of its early settlement in the form of great sepulchral mounds. There were Iron Age lake dwellings, too, such as have left their traces along the margins of the Swiss lakes.

Marseille, now the second city of France and its largest seaport, began as a Greek settlement (Massilia) about 600 B.C.

GALLO-ROMAN

In 121 B.C. the Romans gained control of the Greek port and colony of Massilia. Then, in the middle of the first century B.C., Julius Caesar began his eight-year conquest of a divided Gaul which thus became the first Roman province north of the Alps, one of the richest of the Empire. It was destined to remain under Roman rule until the fifth century when the Western Empire

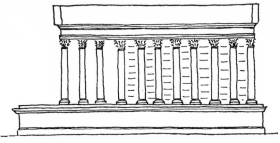

MAISON CARRÉE, NÎMES

began to disintegrate under the assaults of the barbarians from beyond the Rhine and Danube.

The most Romanized part of Gaul, what is now modern France, was the south-east where the Celtic Gaulish language soon gave way before Latin; and it is not accidental that it is in the lower valley of the Rhône that today most of the evidence of Roman occupation is to be found, like the Corinthian columns standing strangely in the fields near Riez and the remains at Vaucluse.

At Nîmes is the famous 'Maison Carrée' (16 B.C.), a small but extremely well-preserved example of a Roman temple. Standing on a podium, its portico entrance reached up a flight of steps, it is what the Roman architect Vitruvius classified as a pseudo-peripteral prostyle hextastyle temple, which is to say it consists of a rectangular *cella* or walled chamber with attached columns and a six-columned pedimented portico. The detailing of the Corinthian base mouldings, capitals, and entablature is of the highest quality.

Also at Nîmes are the interesting remains of a nymphaeum (145) or cool retreat of plants and water (a sort of ancestor of the conservatory), once part of the thermae complex there. Known as the 'Temple of Diana', it is oblong in plan, its interior walls articulated with Corinthian columns – the Corinthian order was always favourite with the Romans – supporting an entablature from which springs a barrel vault with transverse ribs. This was probably the forerunner of so many Romanesque examples to be found in southern France a thousand years later, for Roman temples were not as a rule vaulted. Between the columns are niches for statues, with alternating triangular and segmental pediments. The main vault is abutted by the vaulting of the 'aisles' which flank the inner *cella*, the only lighting for which

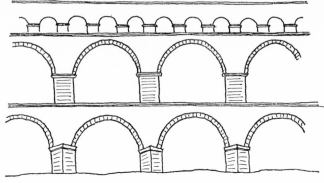

PONT DU GARD, NÎMES

appears to have come from the openings at the end of the barrel vault. The roof extended over the whole width of the building and was stone-slabbed.

Other Roman monuments at Nîmes are the Baths of the Wonderful Fountain and the Tower of Magnus on its wooded hill.

The Pont du Gard, Nîmes (150) is a six-arched bridge that is part of a very large aqueduct which carried water from Uzès twenty-five miles away to the town, over the River Gard. It is one of the finest surviving examples of such works, in which the engineering skill of the Romans excelled. Its structure is a three-tier superimposition of arcades, the highest and smallest bearing the 'specus' or water channel. Its material is unmortared stone, though elsewhere brick and timber were used extensively, the characteristic Gallo-Roman brick being large and square, with quadrant bricks where columns were required. Poitiers has a few arches remaining of the three aqueducts which once brought water to the Roman settlement there.

The amphitheatre at Nîmes is an earlier work dating from about 30 B.C., used much later by the Visigoths as a stronghold and occupied as slums in the last century. Originally its tiered seating accommodated over 20,000 spectators for the bloody spectacles which took place in the arena. The façade is an arcaded design of two storeys with superimposed orders applied non-structurally in the usual Roman manner. Arles to the south-east also has a first-century amphitheatre and remains of thermae, those baths and recreational centres that played so important a role in the social life of the Romans. At Avignon are the remains of another amphitheatre and there were others in the west: Saintes, still used for theatrical performances on occasion, and the one at Poitiers. Designed to seat 40,000, this was the largest after the Coliseum in Rome. Not far away are the impressive baths at Sançay.

Roman Gaul was a highly civilized place despite the harshness and cruelty of certain aspects of its life. Thus the finest Roman theatre in Europe is at Orange (50), to the north of Avignon. The imposing semi-circular auditorium is partly built up on inclined concrete vaults and partly excavated from the sloping ground, which was the practice generally adopted where the terrain permitted. The audience of 7,000 reached their seats by means of radiating stairs leading up through the tiers and all commanded a good view of the large stage backed by a high enclosed proscenium. The back of this block is an arcuated structure and is interestingly fitted with projecting corbel stones pierced to receive the poles of the velarium or awning which sheltered the audience from the hot Provençal sun.

MAUSOLEUM, SAINT-RÉMY

The Roman Empire was, of course, based in the first place upon military might and the triumphal arch was the chief architectural symbol of this. The Arch of Tiberius at Orange (30 B.C.) is of the triple-opening type consisting of a large archway flanked by two smaller ones, its piers ornamented with attached Corinthian columns which appear to carry an entablature and attic above. Other remains of such monuments are to be found at Saint-Rémy – also a small but exquisite mausoleum – Cavaillon, Carpentras in Provence and Saintes in the west.

Vaison in Provence has a theatre, villas with mosaics, and a stone bridge, whilst in the Rhône valley Lyon, once the Roman colony of Lugdunum, preserves its theatre, still used, and fragments of its aqueducts. A road system centred on Lyon was established. Further south the ancient city of Vienne has the temple of Augustus and Livia. From Clermont-Ferrand (Augustonemetum) in the Auvergne may be visited the ruins of the Temple of Mercury Arvernovix on the volcanic mountain of the Puy de Dôme.

Many French towns began as Gallo-Roman settlements, some preserving the impress of their original rectilinear plan of intersecting streets into the Middle Ages. In fact in the street lay-out of modern Paris are traces of the grid plan of Lutetia the buildings of which have almost entirely vanished with the forum that once lay westward of the Panthéon; except for the great vaulted hall which was once the *frigidarium* of the large baths on the site of the Hôtel de Cluny, still an impressive structure. Compiègne, to the north-east of Paris, has the remains of its third-century town walls. Among the most impressive civil and military works are the famous gateways of another town of Roman foundation, Autun, south of Dijon. Here the Porte Saint-André is unusually large since it has two big arched openings for vehicular traffic flanked by the more customary smaller openings for pedestrians. Above these entrances is a gallery of narrow arches between which are Ionic pilasters or, in the case of the second gateway at Autun, Corinthian pilasters. These galleries connect with the rampart walls on either side which, like the top of the gateways themselves, are crenellated in the usual manner of Roman fortification. Reims possesses another interesting example in the Porte de Mars.

Even today Provençal farmsteads echo Roman villa architecture in their pedimental gables and tiled roofs. We know from the descriptions of the fifth-century poet Sidonius Apollinaris, Bishop

PORTE SAINT-ANDRÉ, AUTUN

of Clermont, that there were many Roman patrician estates which supported fine country houses luxuriously equipped with baths and oratories or chapels, whatever the conditions under which the slaves who served them subsisted.

They range from the great complex of Chiragan on the Garonne (40 acres) through medium-sized examples like Montmaurin in the Haute-Garonne to quite small villas. Their rooms open off a corridor or a peristyle and larger specimens are grouped round courts. A fortified villa may be visited at Thesée, not far from Tours. The so-called Temple of Janus at Autun is really a sturdy brick-built tower fortification, like the Tower of Magnus at Nîmes.

Of the sculpture and mosaics which once decorated these villas and the public buildings of the towns, so many of which were destroyed by the barbarians from the fifth century onwards, fine examples may still be seen in the museum of the Louvre in Paris. Next to the Musée de Cluny, also in Paris, are the remains of a palatial Roman residence with baths, while on the hill of Montmartre was a temple.

As has been made clear, however, the main legacy of Rome, architecturally, was bequeathed to the Rhône valley where Roman culture first took root and thrived the longest. It was Provence in the south and Burgundy in the north which cherished its memory latest, as we shall see when considering the Romanesque architecture of these provinces some five hundred years later.

PRE-ROMANESQUE

In the fourth and fifth century the barbarians from across the Rhine began to make inroads into the Roman province of Gaul and finally overran it: Visigoths, Burgundians, Alamans, Vandals, and Huns. Checked by a Gallo-Roman and Visigoth army at Châlons on the Marne (451), Attila and the Huns left the field free for the Franks who had first attacked in the third century. United under Clovis they now founded a Frankish Kingdom with Clovis himself the first of the Merovingian dynasty, and the merging of Gallo-Roman and Frankish elements, as in the language of the people, provided the base from which the French nation was to grow.

When the Franks arrived in Gaul they found it already a Christianized country with basilican churches and baptisteries such as had developed in Italy since Constantine's Edict of Milan had permitted freedom of worship to Christians throughout the Empire. Clovis I was baptized in 496 but even before this apostle-bishops had founded churches at Arles, Clermont-Ferrand, Lyon, Toulouse, and Tours.

St Martin had been particularly active in the fourth century and a large church was built to commemorate him at Tours (472) but has not survived.

Examples from this early period are the fourth-century Gallo-Roman baptistery (where immersion was practised after the Edict of Milan) attached to the small seventh-century church of Saint-Jean, Poitiers, and dating from about the same time, the traces of the basilica of Saint-Bertrand-de-Comminges near Luchon in the Pyrenees, with nave, narthex, and eastern polygonal apse. These early basilicas appear to have been both unaisled and, if large, aisled; sometimes, as at Clermont-Ferrand in the late fifth century, there was a bema, that prototype of the transept. They obviously follow the Early Christian tradition emanating from late Rome, but in a more rudimentary provincial manner and on a smaller scale.

The basilicas would have had open timber roofs; but there were early attempts at vaulting, such as the small fifth-century barrel vaults at the oratories of Sainte-Irénée, Lyon – the basilica itself dated from c. 200 – and Saint-Victor, Marseille, and the sixth-century domed octagon-in-square baptisteries of Provence represented by those at Marseille and Fréjus. The latter was probably a type owing its origin to the Baptistery of the Orthodox at Ravenna but there was now at this time a strong influence from the east, from Syria, and, more indirectly, Africa whence came the monastic system. With them there were important trade connections. These other influences were felt in the design of the fifth-century cathedral at Clermont-Ferrand. It had a prothesis and a

1a. St-Philibert-de-Grandlieu: a venerable ninth-century Carolingian church. All such basilicas had open timber roofs but already the column was giving way to the Romanesque compound pier, here of massive proportions. Remarkable early crypt.

1b. Fontevrault Abbey Church, Anjou (early twelfth century): counter-pointed by the rapid rhythm of the dwarf arcading above, a very tall close-set arcade surrounds the well-lit apse which produces a dramatic effect when seen from the darker nave. Note the carved capitals.

2a. Uzès, Provence: the cathedral and twelfth-century Fenestrelle tower, looking down from the Duché, the formidable castle of the dukes. The low-pitched roofs are characteristic of a Mediterranean region of low rainfall.

2b. Arles, Provence: the barrel-vaulted cloisters of St-Trophime, open in the warm climate, have Romanesque round-headed arches on coupled columns. The sculpture and carved capitals are reminders that this was once the *Provincia Romana*.

diaconium flanking the apse, like a Syrian church; but instead of the usual atrium it had a second apse like the North African churches. External features were campanile, at the crossing or detached, as at Saint-Martin at Tours (rebuilt in 472), another large basilica with aisles and transepts. La Daurade, Toulouse, was circular in plan like an Early Christian baptistery, its very name an allusion to the gilded richness of an interior given warmth and colour by extensive mosaic ornament. This was more than decoration, of course, and gave both mystery and meaning to the interior. Campaniles were commonly a feature from the fifth century, either detached, as in Italy, or over the crossing.

It is evident, then, that during Merovingian times (c. 500–751), architecture in France built under Frankish kings was essentially a Christian architecture owing everything to Roman and eastern influences. Despite the violence described by Gregory of Tours, Gaul had been re-Christianized by Clovis, and most of the great cathedrals and abbeys of France such as those of Paris and Saint-Denis – the bishop-martyr of Paris – were founded during the fifth and sixth centuries. Unfortunately, however, the destruction and the rebuilding caused by constant warfare, especially after the death of Lothar in 561, has robbed us of the riches of the Merovingian period. One of the most interesting of the remains of the later period, however, is the seventh-century Saint-Jean, Poitiers, the early baptistery of which has been referred to. Again it is a basilican church with aisled nave, narthex at the entrance, and apse for the sanctuary.

SAINT-JEAN, POITIERS

Also at Poitiers is the seventh-century Hypogée martyrium; and at Civaux a vast Merovingian necropolis has yielded some 16,000 stone sarcophagi.

Charles Martel preserved France from Islam by checking the Arab advance northwards at Moussais-la-Bataille (732), north of Poitiers, but conditions in France did not become stable until about the middle of the eighth century when King Pépin, the founder of the Carolingian dynasty, united the four kingdoms of the Île de France, roughly corresponding geographically to the Paris basin, into the real nucleus of modern France.

His son Charles the Great, Charlemagne, became King in 771, subdued the German tribes and was crowned Holy Roman Emperor by the Pope in 800. From his reign date important architectural innovations now chiefly illustrated by work done under his patronage at Aachen in the Rhineland, where centralized Byzantine planning and decoration can be seen at the Palatine Chapel (805), inspired by S. Vitale, Ravenna.

In France itself the new basilica at Saint-Denis, consecrated 775, showed the introduction of extended transepts for the first time, while another large abbey church, Centula (Saint-Riquier) near Abbeville (790) was a complex Rhenish design with double transepts, crossing and staircase towers.

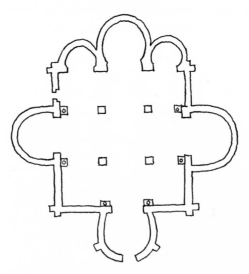

ORATORY, GERMIGNY-DES-PRÉS

Reims had a cathedral as early as 340, but the largely rebuilt early ninth-century church appears to have resembled the Centula with a Rhenish 'westwork', i.e. a low western entrance porch with a chapel over, opening to the nave.

Byzantine inspiration is evidently behind the inscribed Greek cross plan and the mosaics of the church at Germigny-des-Prés, near Orléans (806), a fine monumental design by a Catalan architect. Restored, it is an inscribed Greek cross with apsed arms and a high central dome supported on 'trompes' or squinch arches to carry the transitions from square to circle. The rebuilt Saint-Denis had an apse of horse-shoe shape, but here there are unusual horse-shoe apses on three of the sides and horse-shoe arches in the interior. These are evidence of Islamic influence felt through Spanish architecture from the early eighth century; though the Arabs themselves did not originate the motif and they might have had more significant effect on developments had not their penetration of southern France been halted by Charles Martel. A later oriental influence in the ninth and tenth centuries is revealed in some attempts at small ribbed structures like Islamic domes, for example Sainte-Croix at Oloron in the Pyrenees.

Returning to the earlier Carolingian period and the church at Germigny-des-Prés, which bears some resemblance to the Spanish church of S. Miguel, Tarrasa, it must be said that its centralized Byzantine plan was not much favoured in the west, though it may be taken as a demonstration of the search at that time for new avenues of architectural development.

Other interesting Carolingian innovations were the introduction of the choir, and the ambulatory running round the apse with chapels opening off. It was employed at Saint-Philibert-de-Grand-lieu (c. 840), in the crypt. Being so well adapted to the needs of circulation in large churches it became in later, Romanesque, times one of the two principal ways of terminating the east end – in its fullest development the famous chevet of French Gothic cathedrals.

Saint-Philibert at Grandlieu, now much altered, is also notable for the fact that here about this time the column gave way to the pier; that was to become the characteristic Romanesque vertical supporting member. There is also a Carolingian church, Saint-Martin, at Angers.

Saint-German at Auxerre and the abbey at Jumièges are other examples of early two-tower west fronts and also interesting early vaults, small barrel-vaulted naves with aisles; in the church of the Basse-Oeuvre, Beauvais, there is an aisled nave of the period though the apse has now gone.

Domestic architecture from the Merovingian and Carolingian periods has not survived, being built of timber, like that of the Saxon period in England.

Soon after the death of Charlemagne (814) the Holy Roman Empire broke apart under external assault, and for the next hundred years there was little building work carried out in Gaul. Only with the stability created by the arrival on the scene of Otto the Great were circumstances again favourable to architectural progress. By this time what might be called the pre-Romanesque styles were about to make way for a new mode, the Early Romanesque of the tenth and eleventh centuries, appropriately marking a new millennium and the beginning of the Middle Ages.

CHAPTER TWO

Romanesque c. 1000—c. 1150

By the end of the tenth century the growing centres of modern France, Paris and Orléans, were the domains of Hugh Capet, Count of Paris and founder of the Capetian dynasty which was to last until the fourteenth century. Though Hugh was crowned King of the Franks in 987, for the most part the rest of what is now the land of France was still fragmented, separated into independent territories, and it was this fact that ensured that French Romanesque architecture was not a uniform phenomenon but a collection of regional styles. These were not nearly so clear-cut and distinctive as has formerly been suggested but different enough to justify a regional approach in describing the architecture of the tenth and eleventh centuries.

There are, however, the general characteristics of Romanesque architecture to consider first before we can focus on the regional distinctions and it will be useful to attempt therefore a preliminary brief summary of the Romanesque system of design.

The late tenth century saw a number of innovations in the aisled basilican great churches of the period, usually built of rubble faced with large cut stones, except in those districts like Languedoc where stone was scarce, when brick was the material used.

Firstly, there was a new desire to articulate space by emphasizing bays with piers internally and pilaster strips or wall buttresses at intervals along the walls externally.

Secondly, there were developments in stone vaulting from the middle of the eleventh century when master masons acquired the requisite technology to allow them to vault the naves of larger churches. No doubt the desire to do so owed something to the need to avoid the ever-present fire risks in open timber roofs, but such vaults also helped to unify interior spaces and so further the effects of articulation just described.

Before the high vault was achieved in the eleventh century usually only the aisles were stone vaulted (the crypt of Saint-Bénigne, Dijon dates from 1001), the nave being covered by a timber roof of steep pitch. Vaulting took two main forms, both of them deriving from Roman examples largely neglected in Early Christian architecture: the barrel vault and the cross vault formed from the intersections of two barrel vaults over an oblong or square bay. Barrel vaults were sometimes pointed, to reduce the vault thrust, and sometimes strengthened by transverse arches like massive ribs. Cross vaults were sometimes formed on intersecting segmental ribs following the groins, thus producing the rib vault, a Romanesque invention which became typical of Gothic later on when more complex forms were evolved.

The result was a move forward from the inert stability of Roman vaults towards the dynamic equilibrium of the Gothic vault. Vaulting compartments were usually square, even if this meant putting two rectangular nave bays together to make one, and quadripartite vaults were usually domical, i.e. with the diagonal ribs of the greatest span semi-circular and rising high to the crown of the vault.

Thirdly, towers to dramatize exteriors and bring unity to a grouped composition were made a feature of crossings, west fronts (one or two), and transepts which now became more prominent and sometimes double in large churches. The first and third of these developments may be traced back to the Rhineland; the second – vaulting – is not so easily related to a particular region. Rib vaulting probably began at Durham in 1093, but S. Ambrogio, Milan, also has one of the earliest in Europe. Barrel vaulting, a less complicated form of stone covering, however, was very widely used in France, which still preserves the best examples of this period.

The west front was made a frontispiece to the design as a whole and as well as the twin-tower motif being a common feature – the towers divided into stages – there is the elaboration and ornament of arcading and large portals of round headed arches supported on colonnettes recessed in several orders.

Windows are usually narrow with wide splays and are round-headed too. Sometimes they appear in groups contained within a larger arch, but generally they appear as small openings, especially in the sunnier climate of the Midi, which do not detract from the massive plainness of the side walls and their broad flat buttresses. Solids overwhelmingly dominate voids.

The total impression of a typical Romanesque composition is,

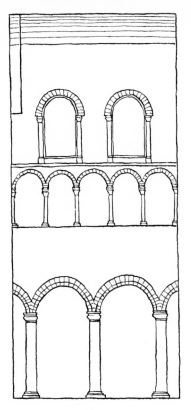

SAINT-BENOÎT-SUR-LOIRE

in fact, one of massive geometrical forms and volumes. In individual members this is reflected in the design of arcade piers to carry the high vault, for unlike the Roman architects the Romanesque master masons made the column once again into a load-bearing structural member. Thus they are thick, heavy, and often columnar, sometimes with attached half round shafts.

With two aisle bays to one nave-vaulting compartment the intermediate piers are lighter and in some instances have attached shafts, as described, running up to support an intermediate rib and thus turn a quadripartite vault into a sexpartite one.

Capitals, including Corinthianesque and cubiform (cushion) types, are strongly carved in varied separate designs favouring stylized animals and leaf forms, and there are carved tympana

over doorways. As we shall see, the south has some fine exceptions, but as a general rule other forms of ornament are confined
to corbel tables fashioned into grotesques, diaper-carved span-
drels, and rather heavy mouldings bearing billet, zigzag, and
rosette motifs. In windows there was some use of stained glass
in the north, though the south did not employ it, preferring the
decorative qualities of fresco painting.

Above all, France evolved the standard plans for the east ends
of Romanesque churches. These were the staggered and the
radiating types. The staggered plan appeared at the first rebuilding
of Cluny (981), the Burgundian centre of the first great monastic
reform of the Middle Ages, which began in 909. It was a centre
of outstanding importance, too, for the evolution of Romanesque
architecture from the tenth century. At the second rebuilding of
Cluny in 1089 it was given much more complex eastern parts
with radiating chapels and in addition transeptal ones. Neither of
these have survived, except for one octagonal west tower from
the second rebuilding, for the abbey was unforgivably destroyed
in 1798.

Another innovation at Cluny appears to have been the adoption
at the second rebuilding of the pointed arch in the long nave
arcade, perhaps for the first time in Europe. The nave was covered
with one of the earliest large barrel vaults in France, and the double
aisles were probably groin vaulted. As the latter were narrower
in span than a timber roof the effect would be to confirm the long
narrow effect of a medieval church interior.

The radiating plan we saw beginning in a rudimentary form in
Carolingian times at Saint-Philibert-de-Grandlieu; but it appeared
above ground at the cathedral of Clermont-Ferrand (964) and
with radiating chapel at Saint-Martin at Tours in 997. The earliest
extant examples of the types, however, are from the beginning of
the eleventh century: Notre-Dame-de-la-Couture, Le Mans, and
Saint-Philibert, Tournus.

Both these varieties of east end were rational attempts to
provide more chapels, now that there was an increasing emphasis
on saints and every priest said a daily mass. At the same time they
provided imaginative terminations to the whole eastward movement of the interiors of great Romanesque churches and gave
structural support to the high vault.

After this short conspectus of its general developments we are
now in a better position to examine the regional expressions of the

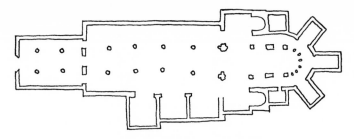

SAINT-PHILIBERT, TOURNUS

Romanesque style in France, starting with that ancient kingdom of Burgundy, which proved to be one of the most varied, inventive, and influential: Cluny is evidence of that.

Saint-Philibert, Tournus (*c.* 1019) is the best surviving eleventh-century church in France, for despite its somewhat severe appearance it was a very progressive design in its day, a monastic church like Cluny, and monasteries were very important in the formation of the Romanesque system. Reference has just been made to its early radiating east end with ambulatory. The nave has a round-arched arcade and transverse barrel vaulting which allows lighting through small clerestory windows; the aisles are also vaulted with transverse barrel vaults and are half-vaulted at the second storey. The barrel vaults in the upper part of the ante-church or narthex are among the first high ones in France and also show the inventiveness and experimentation of the period. In one form or another, barrel or tunnel vaulting was the most characteristic form adopted in French Romanesque architecture.

Though structurally more conservative for its time, following the earlier Cluny in its interior features, Autun cathedral (1132) shows the Burgundian preference for pointed nave arcades – the fluted classical pilasters applied to the piers and to the wall above them remind us that Autun was a town with a Roman tradition – a blind triforium, small clerestory, and over the nave a great pointed barrel vault with pointed transverse arches. The aisles of the basilican arrangement are lower than the nave, of course, and by contrast groin vaulted. The east end has three apses and the west front portals are richly sculptured in the tympana.

La Madeleine, Vézelay, formerly an abbey church, dates from 1096 and has a two-storey elevation (i.e. without a gallery but with a small clerestory) and two-storeyed aisles, similar in some

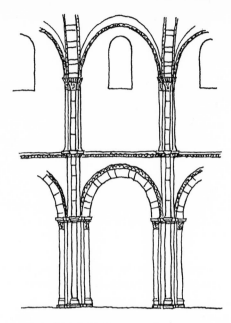

LA MADELEINE, VÉZELAY

respects to Autun; but instead of the pointed barrel vault it has very high domical groined nave vaults between great two-tone transverse arches defining the square vaulting compartments of the long nave.

At the west end it has a striking double figure portal, elaborately carved as was the Burgundian custom except where the puritanical Cistercians were involved, reached through a narthex or galilee of Cluniac origin. This corresponds to the triple division of the main vessel of the church in that it is aisled (the vaults of 1130 are probably the earliest pointed cross vaults in France) and it has three portals, square-headed with sculptured tympana above. Over the centre double portal is a group of five narrow window openings separated by figures, and more sculpture above in the high curved gables which extends between the western flanking towers, only one of which now rises to its proper height.

A special feature of twelfth-century French Romanesque is the type of portal just described. The attenuated stylized figures with small heads are a Spanish type and reappear at the sides of the

LA MADELEINE, VÉZELAY

two portals at Moissac (1115). A little later are those of the Madeleine and the cathedral of Autun. The motif was to become one
of the most characteristic features of the west fronts of the great
Gothic churches of France.

The transepts, choir, and chevet east end at Vézelay are all
of the thirteenth century, but a notable Romanesque feature of
this splendid church is the detailing of the carved capitals, foliate
with figures, of a type of which examples had already appeared
in the mid-eleventh century at Saint-Benoît-sur-Loire (Fleury
abbey church), an interesting church whose double transepts
anticipated those of the great abbey, Cluny III, with a remarkable
eleventh-century tower porch originally three storeys high.

The Cistercian order was founded in 1098 as part of the great
upsurge of monastic energy and was a reforming order which
eschewed elaboration and art in favour of austerity and manual

SAINT-BENOÎT-SUR-LOIRE

labour. The abbey church of Fontenay (1139) is an example of a Burgundian church where the aisles are equal to the nave in height and there is no clerestory. It has the very characteristic square east end and rectangular internal chapels in the transepts; a square-cut stubby termination that the Cistercians took with them wherever they spread to in western Europe. Restoration was carried out early in this century.

Vienne was once the capital of Burgundy and still has the Romanesque abbey church of Saint-André-le-Bas, with its fine twelfth-century cloisters, as well as its cathedral.

We have seen how the memory of Roman architecture was still alive at Autun, but even more than Burgundy, Provence, which had its own unique culture, still possessed the remains of Roman architecture to serve as exemplars and was more open to Italian influence.

But Provence was structurally less enterprising and more conservative than Burgundy in its Romanesque architecture. Church plans were generally simple basilicas; several are aisleless,

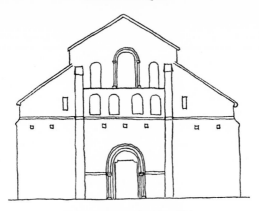

FONTENAY ABBEY

even large ones with flat roofs; but others are tall and narrow with pointed, rather clumsy, barrel vaults over their ungalleried naves, lacking in clerestory lighting, and have half barrel vaults over the aisles, where they are present. Square piers with attached columns are typical.

East ends are usually of the three parallel apse type, but some are polygonal. Towers are absent from west fronts, as is usual

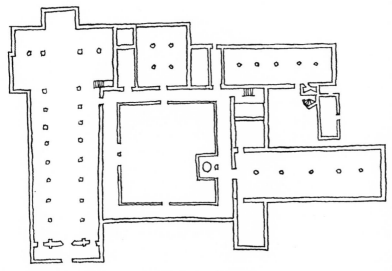

FONTENAY ABBEY

south of Poitou. Their general appearance is well-massed, thickset and sturdy, the towers in particular matching their plain, rather cavernous interiors. But it is in the proportion and detailing, especially in the use of Corinthian and geometrical motifs and sculptural figures, where the Roman tradition can be seen to be most effective. Unfortunately this is sometimes marred by recent embellishments, but not by the modern art additions which are sometimes present.

Saint-Trophime, Arles (1150), and the abbey church of Saint-Gilles-du-Gard not far away and of the same date have finely sculptured façades, the columns and entablatures of which are obviously of Roman inspiration.

At Saint-Trophime the 'triumphal arch' porch has a pediment and deeply recessed jambs to the portals which are of the figured type; Provence has the best figure sculpture in France at this time, stiff and static as it is. Both tympanum and entablature are sculptured too. Here are summed up, in a powerfully moving scheme that is far removed from mere ornamental enrichment, the essential teachings of the early medieval church, and the mood is appropriately solemn and impressive. Saint-Gilles has the most richly sculptured façade of the region, its triple portals linked by colonnades, rather than carved surfaces, in a way that anticipates

PORCH, SAINT-TROPHIME

SAINT-GILLES-DU-GARD

St Mark's, Venice. Saint-Trophime also has graceful Italianate cloisters with coupled columns with elaborately carved capitals; they are open in the southern manner. Saint-Paul-trois-Châteaux, Arles, is another example of Provençal Romanesque, and more are to be found at Notre-Dame-des-Doms, Avignon, with its pointed barrel vault, Saint-Paul-de-Venice, Le Thor (*c.* 1200), and Notre-Dame-du-Bourg at Digne.

Though it cannot be said that this is an arrangement confined to the region, Romanesque churches of Poitou have narrow aisles raised to the full height of the nave giving them a hall-like appearance. It follows too that galleries and clerestories are austerely dispensed with. The early twelfth-century church of Saint-Savin-sur-Gartempe, where in 1835 Prosper Mérimée discovered the famous Romanesque frescoes, is an example of the type with an impressive nave arcade of tall cylindrical piers and three parallel barrel vaults above: a very strong design.

But some churches have no aisles and in others aisle vaults are varied in type. Capitals are, as usual, carved but there is carving on the arch voussoirs too. There are, however, almost no tympana. Some of the finest Romanesque frescoes in France occupy the large interior wall areas. East ends are of the radiating type

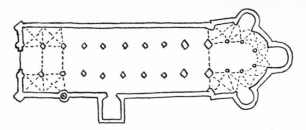

NOTRE-DAME-LA-GRANDE, POITIERS

and there is a tower over the crossing. Following Saint-Benoît-sur-Loire, arcading is used outside and as a sort of triforium.

Notre-Dame-la-Grande, Poitiers (1130) is another church of this Anjou group (i.e. an aisled basilica with a barrel-vaulted nave with bold square) with cut transverse arches, no triforium or clerestory, and a finely executed conical vault over the crossing. It has restored pointed decoration and, externally, a richly carved eleventh-century façade with curious corner turrets, with conical roofs, and sculptured figures in arcaded niches.

Saint-Hilaire, Poitiers, is earlier (1025), with vaulting from the twelfth to the nineteenth centuries. Vienne Cathedral has a notable interior with recessed wall chapels between massive internal buttresses. At Fontevrault Abbey (1101), where two kings of England are buried, Henry II and Richard I, there is an

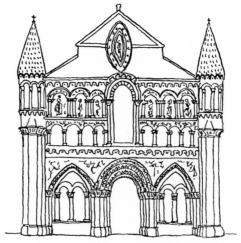

NOTRE-DAME-LA-GRANDE, POITIERS

3. Angoulême Cathedral (1105): a series of domes set on pendentives cover this impressive church in Aquitaine. The grave austerity of its plain surfaces are in sharp contrast to the opulence of any Byzantine analogy which the forms might evoke. The black mortar effect is the result of nineteenth-century restoration.

4. Notre-Dame-du-Port, Clermont-Ferrand: twelfth-century Romanesque in the Auvergne. From the east the composition builds up by stages from the radiating chapels of the chevet. This, the dark stone, low slabbed roofs, and shouldered transept are all characteristic.

SAINT-BENOÎT-SUR-LOIRE, WEST PORCH

interesting monastic kitchen with pointed roof and louvre. In general the church follows the pattern of Angoulême soon to be described.

Other interesting Romanesque churches of the Loire region include Saint-Martin at Tours, Saint-Gildéric, Lavardin (1042) – with early groin vaulting like Saint-Benoît – and the collegiate church of Saint-Ours, Loches (c. 1060), south-east of Tours, with domical vaulting and magnificent pyramidal roofs.

Good tenth-century parish churches are the interestingly planned Saint-Génévoux and the simpler, small church at Autrèche which must have been fairly typical at this time.

D

PARISH CHURCH, AUTRÈCHE

In Aquitaine and the south-west there is a most unusual group of churches of the period. They are usually aisleless – where there are aisles they are as high as the nave – and are made up of domed square bays clearly of Byzantine inspiration. Some have transepts; some have simple apses, some radiating ones.

Angoulême Cathedral (1105) is like a traditional cruciform basilica with long aisleless nave, transepts with chapels and towers (only one of which remains). It is roofed with domes instead of vaults, three on pendentives over the nave bays and a

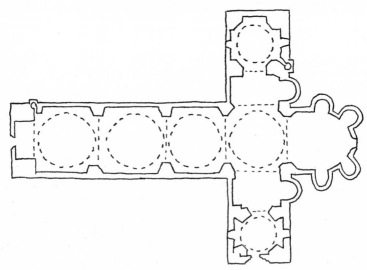

ANGOULÊME CATHEDRAL

double dome on a drum over the crossing. The two-towered façade has five bays of tiered arcades articulated by tall shafts. The upper parts of the towers and gable are pierced by round-headed openings and the main windows are framed in sculpture.

Cahors Cathedral (1119) also has an aisleless nave, and has two pendentive domes. It is perhaps the oldest of the Romanesque domed churches of France, though the choir is Gothic. Solignac has four domes and transepts.

A more interesting plan, and very rare for its time, is that of the much restored Saint-Front, Périgueux (c. 1120). It appears to be modelled on St Mark's, Venice (itself derived from the church of the Holy Apostles, Constantinople), in that it is an aisled inscribed Greek cross with five majestic domes on pendentives, one over the crossing and one over each of the four arms. It has massive arcaded piers and there are an apse and two transeptal chapels. The scale is big and noble and the interior bare and austere, making a striking contrast with the richness one is accustomed to find in a church of the Byzantine type with its surfaces continuously covered with glowing mosaic. Externally, arcading is a decorative feature, e.g. on the apse, and there is a splendid square campanile, detached in the Italian manner, topped by a ring of columns carrying a dome. Périgueux has another Romanesque church, Saint-Étienne (1047).

The abbey church at Souillac, on the other hand, is a basilica with transepts and a splendid apse. The capitals of Aquitaine are Corinthianesque with animals and figures, and in the Charente district this type of ornament is continued, frieze-like, on the

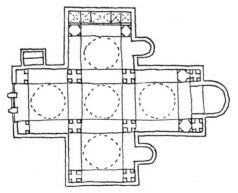

SAINT-FRONT, PÉRIGUEUX

west fronts also. The domed church of Aulnay has a majestic example but the most splendid feature of all is the superb carving of the south portal where the style in which the Romanesque fantasy is expressed resembles that of Byzantine ivories. Its fearsome beasts and apocalyptic imagery remind us that Romanesque carving was not just an aesthetic addition to the architecture but was laden with symbolic, even magical, significance for those who saw life as an unending struggle between the powers of good and evil. In the Pyrenean foothills the cathedral of Saint-Bertrand-de-Comminges (1304) has interesting cloisters, showing that they were not confined to monastic churches.

One of the main influences on French Romanesque architecture cutting across the regional differences so far described was that of the great churches which stood along the pilgrimage routes from Chartres, from Vézelay, and from Arles to Santiago de Compostela in north-west Spain; and along these routes there was interaction between the two countries.

Such churches had high, galleried and barrel-vaulted naves with transverse arches (but no clerestories), usually aisled transepts and radiating east ends, like Saint-Martin at Tours (largely gone). The most important of them was Saint-Sernin, Toulouse (1096) which somewhat resembles Santiago de Compostela.

Cruciform in plan with nave, double aisles, great transepts and large radiating east end, it has nine chapels altogether: five radiating and two in each transept. This gives a magnificent pyramidal grouping of volumes looked at from the east. The barrel

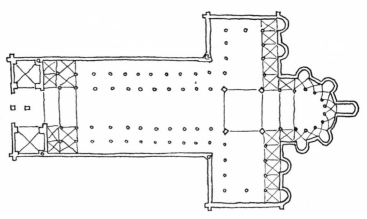

SAINT-SERNIN, TOULOUSE

SAINT-SERNIN, TOULOUSE

vault has square transverse ribs and, since there is no clerestory, lighting is provided through the gallery. The octagonal crossing tower, which set a local pattern, is thirteenth-century and the spire is two centuries later. There is a good deal of admirable sculpture.

Other pilgrimage churches are Sainte-Foyes, Conques (1065) and Saint-Étienne, Nevers (1097).

The pilgrimage type was closely followed in the Romanesque churches of the Auvergne such as Saint-Austremoine, Issoire, the best and largest example; the church at Orcival; Le Puy Cathedral, an aisled cruciform church which, though outside the Aquitaine region, has a nave covered with six domes, all on squinch arches, and Islamic touches; and Notre-Dame-du-Port and Saint-Nectaire, Clermont-Ferrand. Notre-Dame-du-Port has high, two-storeyed aisles that exclude a clerestory and the nave is barrel vaulted with half-barrel vaults over the aisles.

Generally, these Auvergne churches have four radiating chapels in the east end, rather than the more usual three or five, and the inner bays of the transepts are raised to give abutment to the central tower. Columns and capitals are Roman in feeling and there is good detail, often rather profuse. Local characteristics are their gloomy interiors of volcanic stone, despite inlaid decoration of different coloured lavas of the Puy de Dôme district (pumice and tufa – also used for vaulting because of their lightness in weight). Sometimes a stone-slabbed roof of low pitch lies directly on the main stone vault, and an octagonal central power, with curious 'shoulders', half-raised transept to support it and pointed roof, is characteristic.

Before leaving the vicinity of Clermont-Ferrand a most remarkable example of a fortified church might be noted at the nearby spa of Royat. The church itself is a fine Romanesque building, but it has on its exposed side later Gothic machicolated battlements that give it a particularly formidable mien.

Among the founders of the Romanesque style in France were the Normans, who in the early tenth century had come as Viking raiders to pillage and destroy, but who had created the Duchy of Normandy and so rapidly assimilated themselves to French culture that they were soon very inventive and in the van of architectural progress in Europe, despite their somewhat austere and clumsy beginnings. They were the least likely to be affected by Roman precedent and they contributed greatly to the formation of the Gothic style that was to succeed Romanesque towards the end of the twelfth century. Anglo-Norman, however, was important here as much of the most advanced work was carried out in the new churches of England, from which there was a feed-back of ideas and experience to north-west France.

A few eleventh-century Norman churches near Rouen had an ambulatory plan with radiating chapels but the typical plan was what the French term the 'Benedictine plan', i.e. with three parallel apses at the east end as exemplified by the abbey church of Bernay (c. 1000), the earliest example of the Norman school extant. These plans were to be the two alternative solutions passed on to the Anglo-Norman builders across the Channel.

In their developed Romanesque churches the Normans manifested first of all that new sense of space and articulation spoken

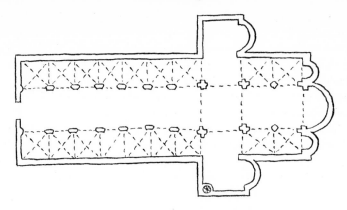

BERNAY ABBEY CHURCH

of earlier. It can be seen at the abbey church of Jumièges (*c.* 1040) and the two abbey churches at Caen where, though they occur in the Rhineland about this period at Speyer Cathedral, for the first time tall shafts appear running right up the interior elevations, dividing them into vertical bay units.

But there are also galleries (not usual except in Normandy and in central France under the influence of the great pilgrimage churches already mentioned), large clerestories marking horizontal diversions and large, steeply-pitched timber roofs to the nave. Naves probably had flat ceilings until the end of the eleventh century saw the introduction of the groin vault and later, after their introduction elsewhere, rib vaults in the early twelfth century, 1110–20.

The church of la Trinité (Abbaye aux Dames), Caen (1062), founded by the wife of William the Conqueror, has one of the earliest examples of sexpartite nave vaulting, since this suited the square nave bays corresponding to two rectangular aisle bays. The lighter alternate piers have shafts carried up to support intermediate transverse ribs thus dividing further what would otherwise have been quadripartite vaults. The thrust of the high vault is resisted by semi-barrel vaults, like concealed flying buttresses in the aisle roof, and carried to the outer wall with its vertical buttresses. The chancel is groin vaulted.

There is a fine two-towered façade; the motif derives from the cathedral of the Alsatian city of Strasbourg (1015), though as we have seen, two-tower fronts go back to the eighth century in

France at Saint-Martin at Autun, Saint-Germain at Auxerre, and at Jumièges. The western towers, which once had spires, are square, like the tower over the crossing, and are divided into arcaded stages with flat buttresses to their angles, similar to those which mark the bay divisions externally at intervals along the massive walls of the church. The entrance is of the triple round-headed portal type.

The Conqueror's church in the same town, Saint-Étienne (Abbaye aux Hommes) 1064, also has early sexpartite vaulting over the nave to replace the timber ceiling, and it may be seen how this has permitted a heightening of the clerestory in a manner

SAINT-ÉTIENNE, CAEN

characteristic of Norman Romanesque and anticipating Gothic developments.

There is a two-tower west front which would have terminated in pyramidal roofs, but which now have beautiful thirteenth-century octagonal spires and angle pinnacles. The octagon above the square crossing tower is also later, and the chevet ending is a twelfth-century modification of the original design.

A third church at Caen, Saint-Nicolas (1084) and the church of the fortified abbey of Mont-Saint-Michel illustrate the difficulties of vaulting before the use of the pointed arch allowed arches of different widths all to be brought to the same height without disadvantage to the strength of the arches and the vault. The cathedrals at Coutances (1056) and Bayeux (1077) are also important designs. That fine Romanesque building continued in Normandy in the twelfth century may be seen not only from the military architecture, the massive donjons referred to later, but in the great vaulted churches like the very accomplished former abbey church of Saint-Georges (1123) at Saint-Martin-de-Boscherville, near Rouen.

General Norman characteristics include a bigness of scale, a massive simplicity, and a preference for rather coarse and frequently abstract geometrical detailing, kept quite subordinate to the structure, however. Caen stone was a superb material, of course, and widely used.

Saint-Rémi, Reims (1005) is another notable northern Romanesque church, but the choir is highly decorative Early Gothic of about 175 years later. In Alsace the late twelfth-century west front of the Benedictine abbey church of Marmoutier, and the surviving eastern parts of the abbey church of Murbach and the handsome Saint-Léger, Guebwiller – both in the Vosges region – with their Lombardic dwarf arcading and geometrical pyramidal capped towers all belong to the school of the Middle Rhine and are clearly more Germanic than French in spirit, like the castle of Kaiserberg overlooking the timbered houses of the little town.

Of twelfth-century monastic architecture, apart from the works already referred to, little has survived the erosion of the centuries and the periodic rebuilding, despite its great importance in the evolution of the medieval tradition. Among the most important survivals are the Cistercian abbey of Fontenay already mentioned: a good specimen of the austere, robust, plain style of that order.

Round the monastic cloisters of Fontenay Abbey were grouped

the conventual buildings, representing the peak of achievement in the domestic architecture of their day and including a splendid square chapter house of nine bays where rib vaulting replaces the barrel and groined vaults of the church and cloisters. Unfortunately, the frater or refectory no longer exists.

In Paris that of the former twelfth-century abbey of Sainte-Geneviève is now the chapel of the Lycée Henri IV and the kitchens are still used as intended. One of the finest French medieval halls to survive, pillared and vaulted, is the frater of the former Benedictine abbey of Saint-Martin-des-Champs, now the library of the Conservatoire des Arts et Métiers. There is an excellent kitchen at Fontevrault Abbey, and there are an interesting fireplace and chimney at Sénanque Abbey, also of twelfth-century date.

Altogether, then, the Romanesque architecture of France is seen to be creative, and innovatory, even though it draws some of its ideas from outside, from Italy, England, and Germany. It is Romanesque not in the sense of imitating antique architecture but in deriving from the structural character of Roman buildings; and it made its own rich contribution to the architecture of Western Europe through a variety of regional styles. In both Romanesque and in the Gothic that succeeded it the French were experimenters and originators, not copyists; this is especially true of the new style of the twelfth century.

CHAPTER THREE

Gothic I

THE main elements that went to make up the new style which originated in the later twelfth century (known as Gothic since the sixteenth century) are each to be found separately in the Romanesque architecture which immediately precede it: the pointed arch, the rib vault, wall and flying buttresses.

The first two structural features were combined to overcome the difficulties posed by rectangular vaulting compartments when

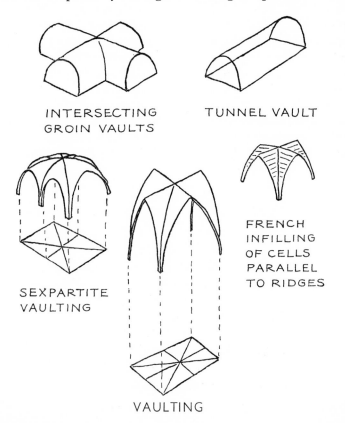

INTERSECTING
GROIN VAULTS

TUNNEL VAULT

SEXPARTITE
VAULTING

FRENCH
INFILLING
OF CELLS
PARALLEL
TO RIDGES

VAULTING

nave bays were made the width of the aisle bays, for by using pointed arches all could be brought to the same height without diminishing the strength of any of them.

Rib vaulting did not originate in France, but in addition to the early ones noted at Caen in Normandy, French Romanesque examples occurred all through at the Abbey of Lessay (1098) and in the choir at Saint-Martin-des-Champs, Paris (1135), which also had a pointed nave arcade. This was the first rib vault in the Île de France, where the Gothic style was born.

The essential feature of the Gothic rib vault, apart from the use of pointed arches, was the separation of the structural member of the rib from the infilling of the panels. The thrust of the high vault so created was concentrated along the ribs and conveyed by flying buttresses over the aisles of the great churches to wall buttresses weighted with pinnacles, and from there diverted to the ground. Thus the new system increased the constructional importance of the buttress. The flying buttress as such was an innovation of Gothic because of the great height of the naves and the width of the double aisles of French cathedrals; and wall buttresses became deeper, often without offsets, so that chapels were sometimes later introduced between them.

Above all Gothic is characterized by the tendency noted in the evolution of Romanesque vaulting towards the creation of a skeletal structure that was in a state of dynamic equilibrium, thrust balanced against thrust, to make a building that was essentially

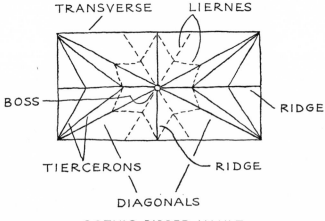

GOTHIC RIBBED VAULT

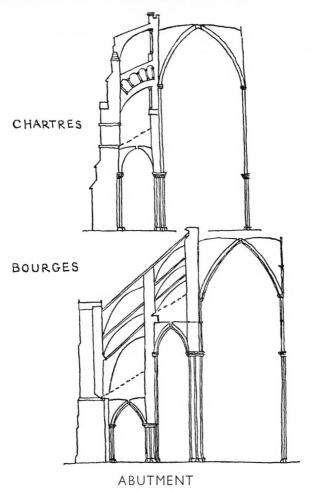

CHARTRES

BOURGES

ABUTMENT

different from an inert classical structure. In such an organic system, more than just the sum of its features, the walls between buttresses – now constructed of smaller stones with thick mortar joints – became less substantial and could be opened up increasingly first with larger pointed windows of the narrow lancet type and then with broader traceried windows, filled with stained glass that was abundantly used from the thirteenth century, its glowing luminous colours giving an added beauty and mystery to the solemn interiors. However much one explains the advent of Gothic in terms of structural development, one cannot overlook the fact that a primary aim was the novel and exciting aesthetic effects allowed by the new system linked to the spiritual aims of the church. It is also a 'logical' style, and historians of ideas might well see an analogy here between structural theory and the twelfth-century rediscovery of logic as an instrument of philosophical dialectic. So too there is a parallel between the new economic and intellectual cosmopolitanism that was abroad at this time and the rapid spread of Gothic from France along the trade routes of Europe to the remotest corners of the continent.

The various tendencies of late Romanesque appear to have crystallized into something different at the rebuilding of the abbey church of Saint-Denis, near Paris (1137) by the splendour-loving Abbot Suger, minister of Louis VII, who helped to consolidate the state and asserted the authority of the crown over the powerful nobles of the realm. Here, in the choir of Saint-Denis, the lower part of which still survives, it may be said that Gothic emerges for the first time as a distinct style, though unfortunately the richness and brilliance of Suger's day have gone.

The massive load-bearing walls of Romanesque were reduced to a new lightness, the thrusts of the elegant ambulatory rib vaults over the interior spaces concentrated on to buttresses to produce the skeletal system just described. The sense of a compartmentalized plan to separate spatial units has gone. Space flows more freely and a subtler and livelier articulation depending on the vaulting has taken the place of the old one.

That this was a transitional work, however, may be illustrated by the conjunction of pointed nave arcade with round-headed windows as at Saint-Germer-de-Fly, near Beauvais, a church of similar period with quadripartite vaults, piers of identical design, and flying buttresses in the aisle roofs. The west front at Saint-Denis continues the two-tower type already imported into the great churches of Normandy.

French Gothic, *le style ogivale*, began then in the north; specifically in the Île de France, now becoming the political focus of the country, where it showed most vitality and spread most. Already the south was well-endowed with Romanesque buildings and the old tradition produced more resistance to change there. Just as the monastic churches had led the way in the evolution of Romanesque, so now the urban communities, which Louis VI and his successors encouraged to offset the political power of the nobles, were mainly responsible for the impetus which produced the great wave of building in the new style that caused about one hundred and fifty cathedrals to be built in the first half of the thirteenth century. These were the centuries (1050–1350) when more stone was quarried in France than in the Egypt of the Pharaohs and the waterways provided a useful means of transport for the immense quantities of material assembled on a cathedral site. Fortunately, there was no shortage of fine limestones in the Paris Basin, a great variety of good freestones being readily available where the rivers had cut down through its gently dipping strata. It was in the quarries that the cathedral builders first acquired their knowledge of stone for they had no real tradition to rely upon. Admiration of their aesthetic and engineering

NOYON CATHEDRAL

achievements should not eclipse the wonderful instinct they developed for the stone itself and its use as a primary material.

The first of the great Gothic cathedrals to be rib-vaulted throughout was Sens (1140). There is strong Norman Romanesque influence in the alternate piers and sexpartite vaulting. Similarly the interior elevation is a three-storey one: pointed arcade, open gallery (as at Mont-Saint-Michel) and a clerestory above. Most churches at this time still preferred a gallery – like Norman Romanesque generally – in a three-storey design. But a few years after, at Noyon (1145), a fourth element was introduced, between the gallery and the clerestory, called a triforium or arcaded wall passage. The introduction of this was a development of considerable importance since it was one of the chief ways in which the solid wall was opened up in the creation of the skeletal system of Gothic structure.

Laon (1160), on its prominent site, got rid of the alternating piers making them all round with varied Corinthianesque capitals; but it still retained the sexpartite vaulting which is typical of French Gothic cathedrals. Like Noyon it has a four-storey interior elevation with triforium, but whereas Noyon combines the

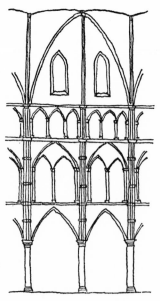

LAON CATHEDRAL

French Romanesque radiating and the German triapsal plan in its east end, that of Laon is unusually square with large lancets and a rose window, the preference being an English one, probably due to the fact that at that time the bishop was an Englishman. Also the transepts at Laon are unusually prominent with later two-storeyed chapels; while Noyon is compact with curved ends to its transepts.

Both cathedrals have impressive west fronts – logical expressions of their basilican interiors, not just 'screens' across the end of the church. At Laon there are three cavernous portals, framed with sculptured saints, already noted in French Romanesque, and square flanking towers, octagonal above. A splendid rose window occupies the gable. Both cathedrals were intended to be seven-towered exteriors: two western towers, two over each transept, and a bigger crossing tower. More than their own Romanesque churches, such French Gothic church exteriors follow the lead of Romanesque development in the Rhineland in seeking a new verticality: the Laon group of towers are the best unmodified

LAON CATHEDRAL

example and probably even they were originally finished with tall un-Romanesque spires.

The porportions of French cathedrals compared with English ones are typically broader, higher, and shorter, partly no doubt because of their cramped town sites but also for reasons of aesthetic preference. Such buildings required a very high degree of structural expertise. Interiors are plain compared with English ones, and because they were not monastic churches – Soissons, an abbey church (1160) is an exception – cloisters are rare. Cathedral chapter-houses, however, became important and are rectangular. Among the best is the double-aisled thirteenth-century chapter-house at Noyon, vaulted in ten bays, and there are also cloisters there.

Notre-Dame, Paris (1163), erected on the Île de la Cité site of a first-century Roman temple dedicated to Jupiter and of a fourth-century Christian church, thus illustrating the continuity of holy places, also has cylindrical arcade piers throughout, with

NOTRE-DAME, PARIS

crocket capitals again, and was designed with an interior elevation of four storeys in which the gallery openings increase from two to three and a row of circular openings replaced the triforium. Now the clerestory windows have been lengthened these only remain to be seen near the crossing, a conservationist idea.

Shafts rise up from the abaci of the arcade piers to the vault, dispensing with horizontal annulets, so that the general direction in which interior design is moving is clear enough: towards thinner members and an opening up of the wall, towards continuous flow, and towards verticality.

Notre-Dame shows clearly too the French preference, compared with the English, for the compact, concentrated plan (the transepts hardly project at all and are almost centrally placed) and the radiating type of east end, though in this case it is not periapsidal but a chevet with chapels between the buttresses of a double ambulatory, a logical continuation of the double aisles of the nave and chancel.

This chevet is the earliest example of its kind, the typical if not exclusive eastern ending to French cathedrals. The ingenious triangular vaulting of the double ambulatory is especially noteworthy. Once again from west to east in Notre-Dame one feels the new spatial flow as distinct from the punctuated effect of Romanesque bays through which one successively moves.

Flying buttresses also appear for the first time at Notre-Dame, and though primarily expressive of structural logic, as we have seen, they also produce rich aesthetic effects which enhance the magnificence of the exterior, particularly when arranged in tiers and crowded round the chevet in a complicated system.

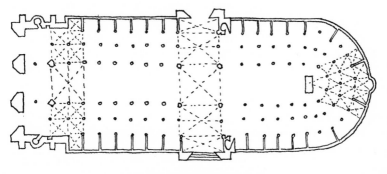

NOTRE-DAME, PARIS

NOTRE-DAME, PARIS

The majestic two-tower west front again has the three deep and elaborate portals with tiers of sculptured figures of saints in niches and, above, a huge rose window flanked by coupled pointed windows contained within pointed arches. Despite the vertical emphasis of Gothic there is a balancing horizontal emphasis in the design – the row of sculptured kings above the portals and higher up the open arcading which ties the gable to the great flanking towers which themselves have horizontal parapets. After *c.* 1220 the straight top finish to a tower became more usual than a spire.

Despite the great weight of masonry in this façade, such is the skill of its design that the impression is of great lucidity and even delicacy. For these reasons it is perhaps the best of all Gothic west fronts; there are others more elaborate.

The gabled transepts have pinnacles and large rose windows, and over the crossing, instead of the great square crossing tower found hitherto, there is an elegant flêche. The crossings of French Gothic cathedrals are as a rule not so distinctly marked as English ones, which being more ramifying in plan require a strong integrating feature at this point. The side chapels between the buttresses are later additions of *c.* 1240.

The cathedral at Nantes (1170) is a smaller, simpler version of Notre-Dame in many respects, but is only a three-storey design thus marking a reversion away from the four-part elevation barely twenty years after its introduction. The stone for Notre-Dame was quarried, like that for Saint-Denis, at Conflans, near the junctions of the Rivers Seine and Oise.

The maturing of Early Gothic into High Gothic is marked by Chartres, rebuilt from *c.* 1194 and dominating the old town. By some this is claimed to be the most beautiful Gothic cathedral in the world. It has a short nave in which Gothic verticality reaches a new height and an aisled transept which is again central, but more traditional than Notre-Dame since it projects appreciably, and a large double-aisled choir and chevet east end over a large crypt of earlier date.

The interior elevational system now becomes a three-storey one, the gallery stage being omitted and the space occupied by it being absorbed by enlarged arcades and clerestory. The triforium takes on a new significance giving increased horizontal unity. This is the revolutionary step taken by that anonymous architect of genius, the Master of Chartres, which becomes the hall-mark of classic Gothic.

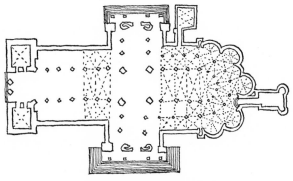

CHARTRES CATHEDRAL

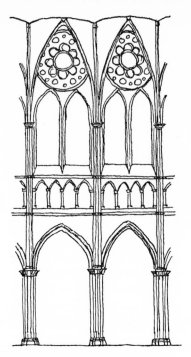

CHARTRES CATHEDRAL

The piers whose centre parts are alternately round and polygonal have now become compound and have their attached shafts carried right up to the vault, which increases the effect of verticality, an important effect of which is to mitigate the impression of weight which the great stone structure would otherwise give. The pier capitals are a carved band.

The diagonal ribs of the high vault spring now from every pier, not every other one, so that the vaulting compartments are probably for the first time rectangular not square, and the vaults themselves are therefore quadripartite instead of the hitherto more usual sexpartite. It follows from this that the spatial rhythm becomes more lively than ever, and the vaults are more logical expressions of the bay system adopted. Lierne and tierceron vaulting had little appeal in France, despite its popularity in English Gothic.

There is a two-tower west front with three richly carved Early Gothic figure portals (the Portail Royal), which are the apotheosis

CHARTRES CATHEDRAL

of those developed in late Romanesque church architecture: long stylized figures with small heads justly renowned for their great distinction, undoubted works of genius. Above are large traceried windows and a large rose window, of which there are other examples in the gables of the transepts. The stained glass of Chartres is of course world-famous. There are 152 out of the 186 original windows remaining. Red, blue, and purple are the dominant colours – the ranges of the latter are particularly splendid – and the result from within is a diffusion of reddish-violet luminosity which fluctuates in intensity and is endowed with almost mystical properties. The north and south transepts also have triple porches, with fine figure sculpture, particularly the north portal, where their freer, more vital, naturalistic but

CHARTRES CATHEDRAL

still immensely dignified feeling contrasts with the Romanesque figures at Saint-Trophime, Arles; though their function is still the same: to instruct, to inspire, and to glorify. Altogether there are 1,800 works of sculpture at Chartres.

A notable external feature is the array of buttresses, especially round the chevet (the ambulatory with its wreath of chapels). They are deep set along the exterior aisle walls with lancet windows between, and a clerestory of circular windows above paired lancets. The flying buttresses spring from towerlike buttress piers and are profusely arranged in three tiers, the original lower two joined by stumpy colonnettes in a very singular but effectively 'muscular' manner (see illustration on p. 37).

The larger but lower twelfth-century south spire is the earliest in France; the other, a richly designed early sixteenth-century example, contrasts with it. Dating from 1507, this represents the culmination of a trend that began at Freiburg Cathedral in 1310 – the gradual dissolving of the unbroken planes of the spire by tracery and the masking of its outlines by pinnacles. With a crossing tower and eastern towers the original design would have had no less than nine towers altogether.

In the first half of the thirteenth century the cathedrals at Reims and Amiens developed the original three-stage elevational systems of Chartres – these three form a closely related trilogy – achieving a dynamic balance between the horizontal progression towards the high altar and the vertical tendency of increasingly slender piers, shafts, pointed arches, and vaults. The proportions are such that the effect is one of increasing height and this is confirmed by the increase in actual height, when measured. The system became standardized in France for about two hundred years.

The second classic of High Gothic is the cathedral of Reims, which inspired Westminster Abbey in London. Severely damaged by the German depredations, the design (probably by the master mason Jean d'Orbais) which dates from 1211 has been extensively restored. Its outstanding qualities are the perfection of balance in the relation of the parts to the whole and its magnificent exterior appearance.

Reims has an aisled nave, with double aisles east of the transept to give more space for the ritual of the coronation of the French kings. The east end is a chevet of five aisles. The interior is of three storeys, as we have said, with clustered piers carrying even slenderer and more pointed arches. It is not only very spacious but also regular and unified.

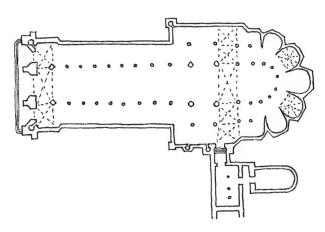

REIMS CATHEDRAL

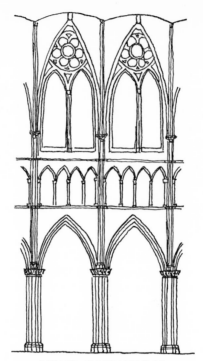

REIMS CATHEDRAL

The two-towered west front by Bernard de Soissons owes
something to Laon but is much more refined and disciplined.
Unlike the other two classics of High Gothic, Chartres and
Amiens, it has its triple portals of deeply recessed pointed arches
arranged in one spread of decoration across the whole width of
the façade. The thirteenth-century sculpture of this elaborate
west front is arranged in a rich iconographical composition with
the Virgin at the centre, figures in the jambs depicting scenes
from her life; while in the three gables of the portals are her
Coronation, the Crucifixion, and the Last Judgment. In the centre
tympana is set a rose window.

There is also a much larger rose window above the central
portal with traceried openings on each side; then a band of sculptured kings in niches binding together the two fifteenth-century
towers (originally spired) with tall openings and angle turrets.
Unlike the western towers of Chartres and Amiens, which are
un-matched, these at Reims really are twin and identical in

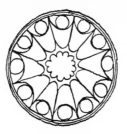

REIMS

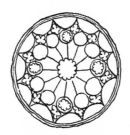

CHARTRES
ROSE WINDOWS

design, and no doubt this is one important reason why the west
front achieves its astonishing sense of poise and balance.

Like painted glass, Gothic sculpture showed the typical medieval use of art to symbolize the function of the church and at
the same time to explain the faith in which it was rooted. The
excellence of the stone carving of the period, however, is not
confined to figure sculpture by any means and can be studied in
the details of pinnacles and corbels, besides fittings like fonts and
tombs. At Reims there are fine examples of refined foliate pier
capitals and subtle arcade mouldings, though as a rule in France
mouldings are usually plainer and less varied than in England.

Though much of the best glass has had to be replaced it was
in the clerestory and aisle windows at Reims that the earlier plate
tracery gave way to bar tracery, which increases in complication at
Amiens (1220) making rich linear patterns, outlining the jewel-
like translucent coloured glass that helped to give a mystical
dimension to the architecture of the interior.

An important aspect of the exterior design of Reims are the
massive tower-like buttress piers from which spring the flying

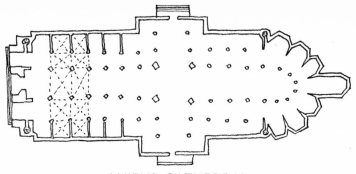

AMIENS CATHEDRAL

buttress. This is like Chartres, but the upper parts are more ornamental with pinnacled tabernacles sheltering angels with outspread
wings.

Like Reims but higher still, Amiens is a very spaciously planned

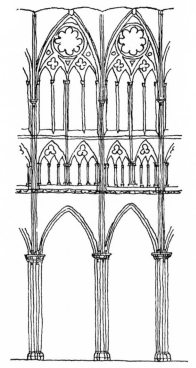

AMIENS CATHEDRAL

cathedral with a wide aisled nave, slightly projecting transepts, a double-aisled choir and a chevet of seven chapels. The triforium of the choir was later replaced by openings corresponding to the main windows, thus showing the tendency to develop voids over solids in the wall areas of Gothic churches.

Altogether this masterpiece of structural clarity, especially the choir, was to prove a very influential design from Beauvais to Antwerp and from Barcelona to Cologne. It is one of the most satisfying of all Gothic cathedral interiors. The cylindrical piers of the nave, which is even more ambitious than Chartres and Reims, have attached shafts running up in what was then the usual way to a very high vault, which makes the roof much too high for any structure over the crossing other than the present tall timber flèche. The triforium stage is noticeably more closely linked with the clerestory than Reims.

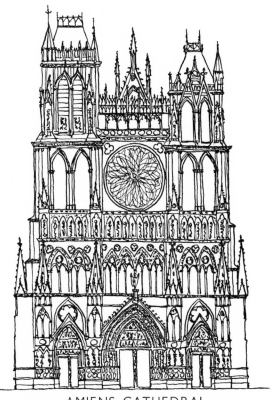

AMIENS CATHEDRAL

The fine west front has splendid figure sculpture and a very notable feature of the interior is the magnificent woodcarving of the stalls. Double flying buttresses divert the thrust of the high vault to the wall buttresses and so to the ground; the chapels between the wall buttresses are later than the main design which is by Robert de Luzarches, though two others also worked on it, showing great virtuosity.

The façade of Amiens – the portals in particular – is replete with stone carving conceived not only aesthetically but according to a carefully worked out iconographical programme expressing the theological doctrine of the church.

Romanesque churches were generally by anonymous architects, by whatever name they went under, ecclesiastical or lay. By the Gothic period we get to know the names of some of the outstanding masters of works who were, not surprisingly, held in great repute. Villard de Honnecourt, for example, probably designer of the last cathedral of Cambrai, who had praised the exterior of Laon as well as the windows at Reims, was a famous thirteenth-century French master mason whose book sheds so much light on the type of men – artist-engineers in stone – who were ultimately responsible for creating these superb structures, whatever freedom was allowed individual craftsmen within that framework. We know the names of five master masons who worked on Reims; at Amiens the nave was the creation of Robert de Luzarches, as we have seen, while the choir and transepts were the contribution of the Cormonts, *père et fils*. Their marks or 'labyrinths' were inlaid in the floor of the nave.

LABYRINTH, REIMS CATHEDRAL

As for the men who carried out these tremendous conceptions, one has only to consider the mastery of the stereometry of stone cutting which the High Gothic achieved to realize the superb degree of skill they possessed, while the sheer scale of the cathedrals relative to the size of the communities whose lives they dominated is still breathtaking today. Amiens covers an area of over 200,000 square feet and could thus accommodate at a single celebration of the mass the entire population of ten thousand.

Soissons Cathedral has a four-storey interior elevation and sexpartite vaults. It dates from 1212 and is even lighter in its effects than Chartres. Like Noyon, it has unusual rounded transepts.

The Cathedral of Saint-Étienne at Bourges (1195), like Chartres, has some of the finest Gothic sculpture and stained glass. A splendid but singular design, it has a magnificent five-aisle lay-out and shows the French preference for a compact plan and broad short nave, like Paris. But there are no transepts and the double aisles are of different heights, an arrangement unique in France. The very tall arcades with attached shafting and the absence of a gallery resemble Chartres; though there is a second triforium in the higher inner aisles between the outer and the main arcades – a much more complex elevation than Chartres – and the nave vaults are sexpartite not quadripartite.

The splendid interior exemplifies the Gothic conception of interior space: layers of space acting as a foil to the masonry structure and absorbing its heaviness into a luminous circumambient envelope.

The two-tower west front, with as many as five round-headed recessed portals, is approached up steps as Paris once was and is a richly decorated composition of niched figures, sculptured

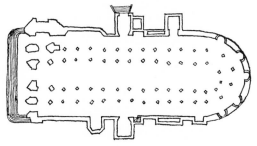

BOURGES CATHEDRAL

tympanum, and rose window frilled with magnificent thirteenth-century stained glass. The side walls are punctuated by typical High Gothic buttresses – deep and pinnacled – from which double flying buttresses leap to take the thrust of the high vault. The roof is characteristically steep, resting on a timber frame that is not now disclosed, since it lies above the high vault.

The great choir of Le Mans Cathedral – all that there is of it – with its splendid chevet of thirteen boldly projecting chapels and cluster of flying buttresses, is of the same date as Amiens and like Bourges appears to be in the same tradition as that of Paris which may have influenced both; but the bare, austere, twelfth-century double-aisled nave is more Romanesque in feeling.

The red sandstone cathedral at Strasbourg in Alsace (1250) has a late Romanesque choir and transepts, but the nave is Gothic and there is a splendid west front, by Erwin von Steinbach, with recessed portals, rose and other traceried windows, and a magnificent single tower (instead of the pair originally projected), the work of two other famous German master masons. It has a delightful octagon and a very tall, open, fifteenth-century spire with incredible spiral staircases. The north doorway, the Portal of St. Lawrence (1495) with its triple-pointed canopy is an outstanding work of its kind. The tympanum, showing the Death of the Virgin in the south transept, is a wonderfully expressive

NORTH DOOR, STRASBOURG CATHEDRAL

5*a*. Carcassonne: with its full complement of defensive features, this is an outstanding example of a fortified medieval town, restored last century. There are two systems of crenellated walls punctuated by towers and gateways of varied form and with typical conical roofs.

5*b*. Hôtel-Dieu, Beaune (1443): a fine late medieval hospital founded by Nicolas Rolin, Chancellor of Burgundy. Notice the galleries, the use of timber, and the huge roof with boldly coloured tiles and dormer windows sporting elaborate finials.

6. Sainte-Chapelle, Paris (1245): Pierre de Montereau's richly decorated royal chapel is a glorious unified space the structural members of which are all attenuated and the walls reduced to screens of stained glass in a logical development of the skeletal system of Gothic.

work of thirteenth-century sculpture beautifully adapted to both its illustrative and architectural roles.

By the mid-thirteenth century a change is noticeable in French Gothic architecture. The transepts and nave of Saint-Denis (1231) – by Pierre de Montereau, master mason of Notre-Dame, Paris, in 1265 and sometimes credited with the celebrated Sainte-Chapelle to be mentioned later in this chapter – have new larger windows, and at Beauvais Cathedral (1247) the shafts of the piers run right up to the vault, uninterrupted by the arcade, and the triforium is glazed; so that the elevation is now two-storeyed without solid horizontal emphasis.

At Beauvais the Romanesque church, 'Basse-Oeuvre', still

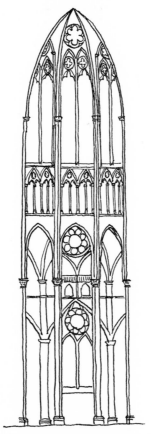

BEAUVAIS CATHEDRAL

stands on the site of the cathedral nave, never completed, and the transepts date from the sixteenth century; but there is sufficient of the choir and chevet of seven chapels, following the example of Amiens, to register unmistakably the new tendency.

The piers are taller, thinner, and more widely spaced; the windows are larger. The vault is the highest ever, 157 feet, no less than three and a half times its span with three tiers of flying buttresses and iron tie-rods are required to ensure its stability. Towards the end of the thirteenth century the roof actually fell in, so far had the Gothic masons overreached their technical skill or caution in their desire for awe-inspiring effects, and it had to be rebuilt in 1337–47 with intermediate piers and flying buttresses. The crossing spire, too, fell in the late sixteenth century, partly because there was no nave to buttress it. Despite its reputation, in terms of mere structure, Beauvais lies behind modern standards; which is only to say that structure, however important, is not all in significant architecture.

The walls between the buttresses are now opened up so that they are a screen of stone and glass rather than a load-bearing wall as in a Romanesque cathedral. The façade of the south transept is as elaborate as some west fronts and is a good example of that late Gothic type of design known as 'Flamboyant' – flowing, sinuous, flame-like tracery that possibly developed, belatedly, from Decorated during the English occupation of the fourteenth century. 'Mouchettes' and 'soufflets', forms of double curves, are much in evidence, though cusps are noticeably absent.

On the other hand, some of the forms of mature Flamboyant are shared with *Sondergotik*, German late Gothic, which is a reminder that we are really concerned here with a style which is a European phenomenon, whatever national characteristics may be recognized and separated.

Flamboyant first appears in France in the Chapelles de la Grange (1373) at Amiens Cathedral and is again seen in the private chapel (1380) for the Duc de Berry at Riom. In both these works there are English elements in vaulting and tracery; the Duke is known to have spent seven years in England.

Another early example is the fine late fourteenth-century screen over the fireplace in the great hall of the Palais des Contes, Poitiers (1384). This is, of course, a secular work and illustrates how forms from church architecture were borrowed for secular purposes so that it became a general style.

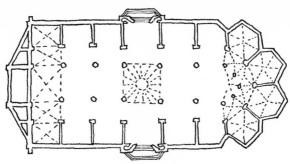

SAINT-MACLOU, ROUEN

But Flamboyant is most commonly found at its best in Normandy. Saint-Ouen, Rouen (1318) has good specimens of window tracery in this manner, besides being an impressive design of pinnacles and spires integrated by a great crossing tower that terminates in an octagon. The enormous west front of the cathedral ranges in date from the twelfth to the sixteenth century, making it quite one of the most complicated, but the great rose window is clearly Flamboyant.

Perhaps the richest display of Flamboyant is to be seen in the late work of Saint-Maclou (1434), in the same city, where the west porch (1500) slopes away in a characteristic late Gothic manner (cf. the choir of Notre-Dame, Caudebec), despite its radiating east and which goes back to an earlier period.

In Gothic, ornament is always more frequent than in Romanesque and favours organic forms, used not only to underline structure but as a more generally applied decoration. This is particularly true of Flamboyant which is essentially a textural style. In fact the label, which derives from the curvilinear type of tracery described above, is applied somewhat superficially at times to work of the fourteenth and fifteenth century as distinct from Gothique à lancettes (lancets or geometrical forms) of the late twelfth and Rayonnant (radiating forms) of thirteenth-century High Gothic. The phases, sometimes referred to as *primaire*, *secondaire*, and *tertiare*, are not, however, neatly confined to these periods.

But mention of Flamboyant as a new element in French Gothic design has carried us too far forward for the time being and we must return to the principal developments noted as Beauvais,

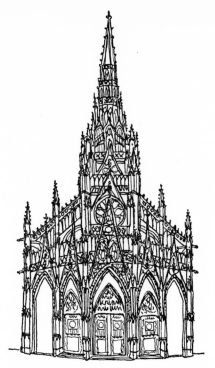

SAINT-MACLOU, ROUEN

where, incidentally, the great doors are a splendid work of Gothic
and Renaissance wood-carving.

The chapel of the French kings, la Sainte-Chapelle (1245) built
by the great Pierre de Montereau for St Louis is a single, aisleless,
high room with virtually all the space between the side buttresses –
there are no flying buttresses – treated as glazed screens, except

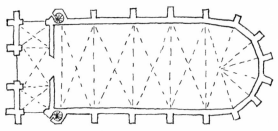

SAINTE-CHAPELLE, PARIS

SAINTE-CHAPELLE, VINCENNES

at the lowest level. Structural members are reduced to the slim-
mest possible and crypt, hall, and apse are all richly vaulted. Here
the logical conclusion of the French Gothic system is reached.

The Sainte-Chapelle, raised on its undercroft to bring it level
with the principal floor, was the forerunner of several château
chapels modelled on it. At Vincennes the Sainte-Chapelle was
begun by Charles v in Flamboyant Gothic towards the end of the
fourteenth century but it was not completed until 1552 when
Philibert Delorme finished the vaulting.

At Saint-Urbain, Troyes (1262) the idea is applied to a great
church. The slenderest of piers have no capitals and the windows,
which fill the wall, are patterned with two layers of tracery of
different design. The flying buttresses, too, are slimmed down to
the minimum.

The intricacy here recalls English Decorated work again;
indeed the first ogee arch is to be found here, though not used

prominently. But it is an unusual effect for France and there are only a few similar buildings, such as the choir of Saint-Nazaire, Carcassonne (c. 1270), and Sées Cathedral of about the same date. It is clear that when the limit of structural development was attained interest was diverted into the creation of much elaborate detail, some of it very rich and attractive, some superabundant to excess. Pendant vaulting, carved bosses, and deeply cut mouldings are all features, and colour was applied not only in the form of diaper wall decoration but also as embellishment to carvings.

Saint-Urbain is famous for the beauty of its western portals and there is a spacious thirteenth-century cathedral in the same city with stained glass from the thirteenth to the sixteenth century, for Troyes was famous for its workshops during all that period. La Madeleine, another of the several Flamboyant churches of Troyes, is noted for its rood-screen (1508), a magnificently rich late Gothic design.

But generally by the third quarter of the thirteenth century French initiative had slackened and later buildings, like the cathedrals of Clermont-Ferrand (1248) and granite Limoges (1273), were content to follow the example of Amiens and Beauvais; Bayonne with its Gothic cloisters follows Reims. Limoges, Clermont-Ferrand, and the splendid red sandstone cathedral of Rodez are all associated with one Jean Deschamps who seems to have been particularly influenced by Amiens. But because of its wealth of Romanesque churches the south, as we have said, has much less Gothic work; though it knew the rib vault as early as 1120 in the porch of Moissac. Toulouse Cathedral, Saint-Sernin, has a large Gothic nave (1272) – the first great Gothic structure in the south – late perhaps because of strong Romanesque inertia (Roman tradition still echoed in the south in the piers of square section with attached columns), and it has a Gothic tower and spire.

Though regional differences during the early Gothic period were not nearly as marked as they had been during the Romanesque, Normandy liked spires – witness Coutances Cathedral (1254) overlooking the sea, where the choir resembles Amiens, with its octagonal lantern over the crossing, its western towers and spires soaring up from the hill on which it stands. Normandy also kept its preferences for galleries (e.g. La Trinité, Fécamp, and Rouen Cathedral (1202), with its 'simulated' gallery), tall triforia, acutely pointed arches, rather than the three-centred arches of late

Gothic, and square crossing towers with spires. The 'bell' capital without foliage and with a round abacus is also a local feature.

Burgundy too favoured galleries and triforia; and very thin detached shafts (e.g. at Auxerre *c.* 1215 and Notre-Dame, Dijon, 1230). Burgundy was much under the influence of the Cistercians who early adopted the rib vault. Where their severity prevailed simpler two-storey elevations excluded the triforia, towers were shunned, and short, square east ends were adopted. Later more complicated forms were tolerated, like the radiating chapels which, with the three-storey elevation, had always been employed by the Benedictines as in the rebuilt abbey church of Vézelay (1160). Nevers Cathedral shows the same contrast between thirteenth-century nave and fourteenth-century choir as at Amiens.

Poitou and Anjou – Plantagenet France – still preferred a hall type of church with high aisles, as at the cathedrals of Poitiers (1162) – with its unusual square east end like that of Dol in Brittany – and Angers (1150), and at Saint-Serge, Angers (*c.* 1200), a particularly fine smaller design. The four-squareness of the two cathedrals and their domical rib vaulting are essentially Romanesque, with a little deference shown to Gothic proportion and spatial feeling.

But originating quite early in that part of the Loire Valley under English kings it really constituted a distinct regional version of Gothic – Angevin Gothic – characterized by a massive-walled broad, 'cubical' type of design which nevertheless absorbed the various vault thrusts in a truly Gothic system. Saint-Serge and the abbey church at Candes, both about 1200, show the rapid refinement of this individualistic manner.

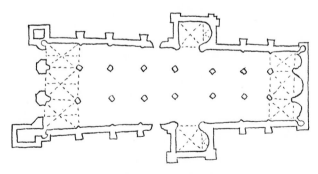

POITIERS CATHEDRAL

Other good Gothic churches so far unmentioned are Bayeux Cathedral (1150), with its huge crypt dating from the eighth to the eleventh centuries, numerous chapels, and octagonal lantern over the crossing; Lisieux Cathedral where the absence of capitals is a noticeable late Gothic feature; Notre-Dame-de-l'Épine, near Châlons-sur-Marne; and the Breton Cathedral of Saint-Pol-de-Léon.

Late Gothic developments were towards greater breadth and plainness in some continental countries, and this tendency may be observed in France in addition to the tendencies already described; though hall-churches were rare except as noted in Poitou which had already a strong tradition in this respect. Solesmes abbey church is a mid-fifteenth-century example of the type, however. It can be related to the growth and multiplication of friars' churches. The two main mendicant orders, the Franciscans and the Dominicans, had been founded in the early years of the thirteenth century and at first they made do with existing buildings. But soon a characteristic type began to emerge, essentially a large plain preaching hall with wide nave with slender piers and wide bays, aisles – where they exist (the Franciscans preferred to dispense with them) – integrated with the nave into one great space, and an absence of eastern chapels.

Though there was no standard type, several variations may be recognized, an interesting example being the high double-naved church of the Jacobins, Toulouse (c. 1260). Now part of the Petit Lycée, this fine chapel, chapter house, and frater of about 1300 – relics of the old Dominican monastery – are probably the best extant examples of friars' architecture in France. The double-aisled type possibly developed from the refectory-type of building. The aisleless hall undoubtedly influenced the evolution of the hall-type church in the south and may have derived from the Cistercian dorter.

Despite its narrow bays and polygonal east end and radiating

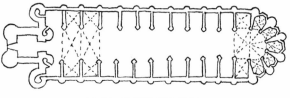

ALBI CATHEDRAL

chapels, the original plan of Albi Cathedral (1282), with its high aisleless vaulted hall interior, the widest in France, and lateral chapels between internal buttresses shows the influence of Catalonia, dominated at this time by the architecture of Spanish friars' churches. Its great fortress-like exterior, too, has the characteristic plainness that is in such strong contrast to High Gothic. But there is also some Flamboyant work in the south porch and an ornate vaulted rood screen. Both the Jacobin church, Toulouse and Albi Cathedral are fine examples of the French medieval use of brick construction, especially in Languedoc and in the Flemish region.

Thus Catalan Gothic, Romanesque, and Cistercian influences chime together to create a very original broad 'horizontal' style characteristic of the south. It may be noted also at Perpignan Cathedral (1324) and in the parish churches of the new towns of the south-west, soon to be described, where fashion and the desire for economy went hand in hand.

Generally late French Gothic was little interested in spatial innovation. There are the hall-churches of La Chaise-Dieu in the

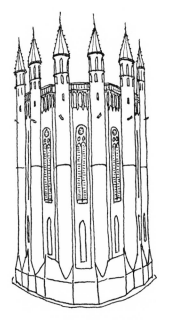

APSE, ALBI CATHEDRAL

Auvergne (*c.* 1342), and the east end of Saint-Séverin, Paris (1489) is of the hall type; but it still retains the ambulatory and radiating chapels of three centuries earlier. So does Saint-Maclou, Rouen, already mentioned in connection with Flamboyant.

In the fifteenth and sixteenth centuries this is not confined to sinuous flame-like linear designs deriving from the ogee or arch of double curvature but implies constructional characteristics too. As we have seen the pierced triforium disappeared generally, leaving only nave arcade and clerestory; very slender piers dispense with capitals, and shafts run right up into the vaulting which often has extra ribs inserted to produce star vaulting, the junctions being marked with prominent bosses. Arches and vaults are noticeably more depressed than before.

Saint-Séverin is one of the finest Flamboyant churches of France, as are Saint-Germain-l'Auxerrois and Saint-Étienne-du-Mont, both in Paris also. All have reminiscences of Notre-Dame in their double aisle plans, retention of triforia, and ambulatory vaulting.

Saint-Maclou, Rouen (1434) shows the tendency for the triforium to be retained also in the Flamboyant churches of Normandy, e.g. Notre-Dame, Caudebec (1426), where the west portal is a superb example; Notre Dame, Alençon; and the granite choir of the abbey church of Mont-Saint-Michel.

Other Flamboyant work may be studied at Saint-Vulfran, Abbeville (1488), parts of Notre-Dame-de-l'Épine (1410), near Châlons-sur-Marne, and the majestic mid-fifteenth-century façade of Toul Cathedral by Tristan d'Hâttonchâtel. Among late examples are the outstanding rich porch of Notre-Dame, Louviers (1510), not far from Rouen; the magnificently decorated Belgian design at Bron (1513) with its wonderful tomb of Margaret of Austria; and the sixteenth-century but still Flamboyant (except for the west front) cathedral of Sainte-Marie, Auch, a very interesting and original late Gothic design in the south. Saint-Jacques, Dieppe, with its three chapels for the local ship-owner, Anzo, shows late Gothic transitional to Early Renaissance.

Reference has already been made to friars' architecture and to some Cistercian abbeys. But of Gothic monasteries a rare and fine example is that of Mont-Saint-Michel, a fortified Benedictine abbey on its massive rocky islet off the coast of Normandy. A place of pilgrimage from its foundation in the eighth century until suppressed in 1790, the existing structure has a twelfth-century

Romanesque nave and a fifteenth-century Gothic choir and was restored in the last century.

Instead of the usual lay-out of buildings on one level the restricted site has led to the novel solution of building upwards in three storeys with the fine church and its fine spire rising grandly from the top. The *Merveille* and the *Salle de Chevaliers* are of very striking appearance and there are fine cloisters as well as secular buildings within the walls of the close-packed complex.

Pontigny, with its very interesting church (1150) showing the transition from Romanesque to Gothic, is a Cistercian abbey in Burgundy. Also in Burgundy is the Carthusian monastery of Champmol in Dijon, with its sculptures by Claus Sluter.

Unfortunately, monastic Gothic elsewhere tends to be fragmentary, and the fifteenth-century Carthusian church of the Grande-Chartreuse, just north of Grenoble, and its mostly seventeenth-century conventual buildings are too large to be typical of that order. The smaller charterhouse of Saint-Sauveur at Villefranche-de-Rouergue (1450), not far from Rodez, gives a truer picture of the general arrangements: a small cloister with kitchen and cellarium, and a great cloister with the cells of the solitary brethren ranged round. Between the two cloisters was a small simple church for common worship, appropriate to this severe and exacting order. More complicated, but clearly of the same family, is the charterhouse at Villeneuve-lès-Avignon, the home of the famous fifteenth-century *Pietà*.

At Laon is a chapel of the military order of the Knights Templar. It is circular in plan since the Order adopted this form after the Church of the Holy Sepulchre, its own headquarters being on the site of Solomon's Temple in Jerusalem. But round plans are rare in medieval architecture and are hardly found after the twelfth century. The church of Neuvy-Saint-Sépulcre is for this reason particularly interesting as a pre-Renaissance centralized church, and a purely round one at that.

CHAPTER FOUR

Gothic II

THE bulk of medieval architecture anywhere is ecclesiastical, but since the Middle Ages were violent times as well as devout ones there was much military building. Unfortunately, the long conflicts under which France suffered, such as the Albigensian War in the thirteenth century and the Hundred Years War (1337–1453) – though being in the first place one cause of them – have deprived her of some of her finest examples of fortification. Many were demolished or converted into residences on the particular orders of Cardinal Richelieu, anxious to frustrate the ability of the magnates to disrupt the Kingdom, as they did in earlier times.

Castles were generally built on some strategically placed site, say on a height overlooking a valley route of importance. The timber structures of Merovingian and Carolingian times, the prototypes of the palisaded motte and bailey castle as depicted in the Bayeux tapestry, e.g. Dinan and Dol, have all gone.

The first stone-built donjons or keeps, rectangular or square on plan and four-storeyed, with the entrance on the first floor, seem to date from the tenth century. Walls were thick with angle buttresses and small openings. The earliest known example is that of Langeais on the River Loire (992). An eleventh-century example is that at Beaugency, also on the Loire. This belongs to the established plan of square or rectangular type, but the twelfth century saw the early innovation of stronger round donjons or polygonal ones, as at Gisors in Normandy, besides the continuation of rectangular plans. At Gisors a chapel dedicated to St Thomas à Becket, once an exile there, was later added and a second wall and towers by Philippe-Auguste. Falaise, also in Normandy, resembled twelfth-century keeps in England.

The most interesting type of fortification belongs to the thirteenth century, however, when the so-called concentric system was adopted. An inner bailey contained by a towered curtain wall was often surrounded by an outer bailey with a lower curtain wall with mural towers and gatehouse entrance equipped with draw-bridge over the encircling dry or wet ditch or moat.

This was a system copied from the Turks during the Crusades which began with Godfrey de Bouillon's expedition in 1096. They had it from the Byzantines who were carrying on the tradition of the late Roman Empire. Krak des Chevaliers in Syria was a Frankish castle. Ideally the system is a symmetrical and truly concentric arrangement, as witnessed for instance in the castle of the Louvre and in the castle of Dourdan, both built by Phillippe-Auguste, rival of Richard 1 of England: squarish on plan with central twin-towered gatehouses and round angle towers at the four corners, the design unmistakably echoing that of Roman forts. But sometimes baileys were arranged next to rather than around one another, as at Coucy on the Aisne (1225), the greatest of all but now unhappily lost for ever. It retained also a great donjon tower.

One of the earliest of these concentric castles is the Château Gaillard, Les Andelys (1196), built by Richard Cœur de Lion to control the Seine Valley, though little remains of it today. It had double curtain walls and a huge circular donjon across the

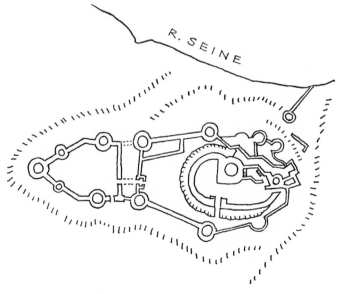

CHÂTEAU GAILLARD

CHÂTEAU GAILLARD: DONJON RESTORED

inner bailey. At the head of the elevated site on which it stands is a separate triangular defensive structure.

Angers has a fine concentric castle of the 'crusader' type built by St Louis. It had seventeen mural towers and two gatehouses. The tall roofs have gone but one can still see the interesting decorative use of stone – chalk banded alternately with a hard shale. Additions in the fifteenth century were a small, more comfortable residence in keeping with the time, and a chapel. Being an important town from an early date, Angers was protected by town walls and the first ramparts are actually Gallo-Roman.

Other well-known fortresses include Najac, mid-thirteenth century, commanding the River Aveyron, with three curtain walls – two running together – the inner one enclosing buildings surrounding an inner courtyard where there was a square residential building and a large round tower, projecting, which served as donjon on principal defensive structure. Though later altered, the royal château of Dourdan, as built in 1222, had a square court, mural towers, and a corner donjon. In the fifteenth century it was owned by the Duc de Berry and is depicted, as it then was, in his famous *Très Riches Heures*. There are Senlis and La Roche-Guyon in the Île de France and several interesting

FOIX

castles along the valley of the Dordogne, such as Val and Anjony, with characteristic circular towers, and along the upper valley of the Lot. There is a famous group of Gascon castles: Larresingle, Terraube, and Massencôme, massive oblong structures marking the old boundary of English occupation, and there are impressive feudal strongholds in Languedoc too, at Aguilar, Opoul, and Quéribus. The castle at Foix in the Pyrenees, with its three

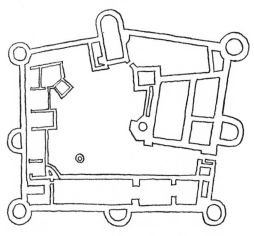

CHÂTEAU DE PIERREFONDS

CHÂTEAU DE PIERREFONDS

towers, is a picturesque specimen. But one of the best known examples of all French military architecture is the magnificent Château de Pierrefonds (1396) near Compiègne in the north. Heavily but effectively restored in the last century by Viollet-le-Duc, this shows the late medieval trend towards a more compact design. On its site above the village, high walls with round corner and mid wall towers – all crenellated and machicolated – enclose an irregular quadrilateral courtyard into which the donjon projects internally. The most genuine part, as distinct from Viollet-le-Duc's 'romanticization' is the north-north-east front by Jean le Noir where the later medieval concept of horizontal line defence may be studied in the two storeys of the curtain wall and double crenellation of the towers, the lower level of the latter corresponding to the upper of the curtain.

A little to the south of Pierrefonds are the impressive ruins of the once great fourteenth-century fortress of La Ferté-Milon (1393) with its great gatehouse and elaborately machicolated towers. At Tarascon, not far from Avignon, is the impressive fifteenth-century fortress of King René overlooking the River Rhône.

A magnificent high donjon is the principal feature of Vincennes (1336), a royal keep surrounded by a curtain wall: the theme, in contrast to Pierrefonds, is an old one.

The Château d'Amboise (1434) on the Loire has interesting Early Renaissance additions and the Early Renaissance châteaux will be described later. But the change from military fortress to residence began in the fifteenth century, by which time firearms had reduced the military function of the castle; though at Chau-

7. Amiens Cathedral: the thirteenth-century portals celebrate the marriage of architecture and sculpture in the service of the Church.

8a (*above*). Boule d'Oz, Bourges:
late medieval vernacular where
timber is exploited to produce
patterned texture. Note the
carved detail and the gable of
distinctly Gothic aspect.

8b (*right*). Hôtel de Sens, Paris:
late fifteenth-century residence
of the archbishops of Sens.
A complex round a court cut
off from the street; an urban
transposition of the country
house plan. Note the
corbelled turrets.

mont and Ussé, both from the last quarter of the century (despite the large windows, dormers, and chimneys which signalized increased domestic comfort) crenellated and machicolated walls and towers still survive, largely for reasons of prestige. Chaumont, especially, with its staircase towers, arcades, and galleries shows the new openness and domestic ease. Yet already Plessis-lès-Tours (1463) was a proper country house, not grim and closed but cheerful and outward-looking with many windows and pointed dormers. The *château de plaisance* has evolved from the *château fort*.

Other transitional examples are the Château d'O, Mortrée, Normandy, and the Château de Châteaudun, rebuilt in 1441, and there is some thirteenth-century work (Salle des États) at Blois.

In Brittany the Château de Josselin is a notable castle going back to the twelfth century but rebuilt in the early sixteenth century, when large mullioned windows were inserted and steep dormered roofs added as the austere fortress gave way to a country house of greater domestic convenience and comfort.

Despite unsettled conditions before the Middle Ages, towns were largely without defensive walls until the beginning of that period. Medieval town fortifications take advantage of natural features of the site, with the result that as a rule the perimeter is much more rounded and less rectangular than the outline of Roman town walls. Though nucleated and irregular in shape – with certain exceptions to be discussed next – medieval cities were walled and expanded at intervals by taking in suburbs which had grown up outside them. Thus the districts of Sainte-Geneviève and Saint-Germain, originally the settlements that the abbeys of that name had attracted, became absorbed into a medieval Paris which from *c*. 1200 had spread outward from it protected kernel on the Île de la Cité.

Inevitably in those days there was for the most part a sharp distinction between town and country, and there was a sudden transition to the fields immediately beyond the walls. Streets were irregular and narrow with jettied houses crowding over them. But behind were courts and cultivated plots which introduced an element of space, a little light and air that were absent for the most part until the advent of the square at the end of the sixteenth century.

From the thirteenth century date a number of towns in the south-west, the products of special circumstances, when that

region was torn by the wars of the Albigensian heresy which
enlarged France at the cost of destroying the distinctive Provençal culture. Guarded by crenellated walls, gatehouse, and
mural towers from which cross fire could be directed, these so-
called 'bastides' were of a semi-military character. They are regularly planned and their streets are noticeably wider than was
usual in the Middle Ages; and a public square was provided at the
centre of the lay-out, a feature uncommon before the seventeenth
century, with a few exceptions.

Though building plots were always rectilinear they varied in
size, e.g. Sainte-Foy-la-Grande, and some were square, like
Mirande. As there were over two hundred bastides they were not
standardized. Other examples are Montauban and Villefranche-
de-Rouergue, which became important regional centres, Créon
(Gironde) and Montflanquin (Lot-et-Garonne). The squares of
Montauban and Sainte-Foy-la-Grande are now typically arcaded
with entries from the corners.

Both Aigues-Mortes and Carcassonne – also much restored in
the nineteenth century by Viollet-le-Duc – show a reversion to

CARCASSONNE

Roman symmetry in their adoption of rectilinear street planning. The former has fifteen mural towers projecting and round, except for the tower of Constance which preceded the town. The latter has two systems of wall defence and some fifty towers, square, round, and semi-circular to the field, and heavily defended gate-houses – all enclosed by a moat.

Monpazier, in the Dordogne, founded in 1284 by Edward 1 of England, has a grid plan, arcaded market place, and impressive fortified walls and towers. The English kings, of course, held land in France from the Conquest until the end of the Hundred Years War in 1453; though Calais was retained until the sixteenth century.

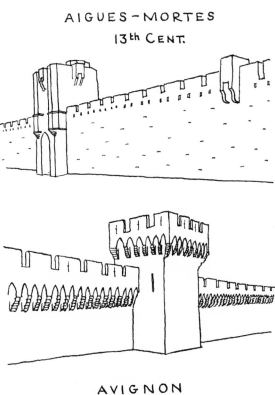

AIGUES-MORTES
13th CENT.

AVIGNON
14th CENT.

FORTIFICATION

Among the best examples of medieval town fortification are those of Villeneuve-lès-Avignon, with the Porte Saint-André, a fine gatehouse with two deeply machicolated round towers dating from the early fourteenth century, and Avignon, where the popes resided at the Palais des Papes from 1307–77 during the period known as the Babylonian Captivity.

Interesting examples of hill-top towns where the houses are arranged in a ring also occur in Provence (e.g. Tourettes-sur-Loup). One result of this was that market taxes, *octroi*, could be better exacted from the peasantry bringing in their produce from the surrounding countryside.

In the fifteenth century a number of Breton towns were fortified, e.g. Saint-Malo, Mont-Saint-Michel, picturesquely rising from the sea, Dinan, and Vannes. Paris has a few fragments from

HÔTEL DE VILLE, DREUX

Charles V's time, for example the Tower of John the Fearless, rue Étienne-Marcel.

Meanwhile there was the civic and domestic architecture of the Middle Ages. Of these categories undoubtedly some of the grandest buildings were some of the large hôtels de ville or town halls which the prosperous cities of the fifteenth century produced, especially in the north where the gilds of industry and trade flourished. But they began in a somewhat extempore fashion, as when the municipal council of Paris took over a nobleman's house in the Place de Grève in the thirteenth century; only later were purpose-built town halls designed.

Compiègne is a fine fifteenth-century Franco-Flemish Flamboyant example: a beautiful symmetrical façade with mullioned and transomed windows, high roof with pierced parapet, dormer windows, corner turrets, and a high central belfry. Bourges too has a fine octagonal tower, Flamboyant in style, and an unusually massive chimney-piece.

Of sixteenth-century examples Saint-Quentin and Dreux are impressive, the latter a square 'tower' with a pyramidal roof, corbelled turrets, and mullioned and transomed windows of the type seen at Compiègne. Beaugency has small but beautiful example, showing the transition to the Renaissance style, dating from 1526. The essential elements of such buildings were a council chamber, a balcony for addressing the citizens, and a belfry for civic prestige and as a symbol of authority. Clocks were a feature from the fourteenth century.

Some of the larger hôtels de ville were equipped with kitchens and chapels, such as that of Arras, the finest of all. Owing something to Saint-Quentin, it was a work of the sixteenth century but was rebuilt to its original design after its destruction by the Germans. Above a ground floor arcaded loggia is the great hall at first floor level, with large traceried and crocketed windows with balconies and round openings over. There is a central balcony and a pierced parapet, above which rises a very steep roof of rich appearance, punctuated as it is by the rhythm of three rows of pointed dormer windows. There is also a tall and magnificent belfry nearly 300 feet high and dominating the Petite Place.

Noyon, Douai, and Valenciennes are others in the north, less grand; and there are interesting examples at Orléans, Angers, and Saumur in the Loire Valley. Orléans resembles Compiègne with modish Italian decoration added, typical of the early sixteenth

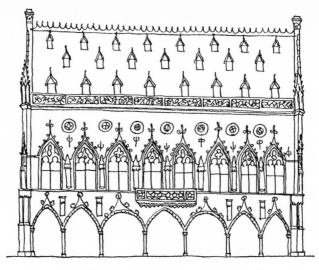

HÔTEL DE VILLE, ARRAS

century. In smaller towns municipal business was commonly carried on in the church as the principal building of the settlement and natural focus of community life.

Despite the very active trade of northern France in the Middle

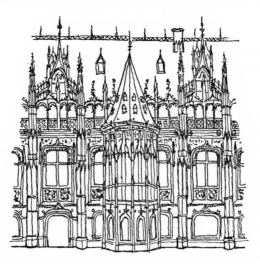

PALAIS DE JUSTICE, ROUEN

Ages, however, nothing remains of the halls of the merchant gilds. In the south at Perpignan the late fourteenth-century Loge de Mer was a medieval exchange-cum-warehouse of a type then found in Catalonia; but it has since been drastically altered. The medieval fortifications of Perpignan have gone, but there are still the Castillet, the citadel, and a fourteenth-century aisleless cathedral.

With the same group of civic buildings we can include the Palais de Justice, the old Treasury, at Rouen, built in 1499 though much restored at the end of the nineteenth century. A large splendidly rich Flamboyant design, it has large mullioned and transomed windows on the first floor, a central octagonal tower with traceried windows and pointed roof, a steeply pitched main roof, the lower part of which is screened with a pierced parapet and openwork stone cresting, pinnacles, and figure sculpture. All this complication and elaborate fantasy makes the building a worthy symbol of the rich and ancient town of Rouen; but as the feudal system had so tight a grip on France, despite the efforts of French kings to encourage the development of towns, it was not usually until the later Middle Ages that municipal life was strong enough to sponsor such fine specimens as this.

Earlier than all these examples of secular Gothic architecture is the great hall called the Salle Synodale, built about 1240 as part of the palace of the Archbishop of Sens. Technically not a civic building, its function was sufficiently similar for it to be bracketed with those just described. An unusual and interesting building is the rather Italianate Gothic royal mint at Figeac in Aquitaine, the Hôtel de la Monnaie (1346).

Good examples of medieval markets, usually large wall-less sheds with barn-like roofs on posts or stone piers, and perhaps gables, are Égreville, Saint-Pierre-sur-Dives, and especially the fifteenth-century market at Crémieu, a fine three-aisled design. Often, however, they were only timber galleries set against the walls of the church as at Bar-sur-Aube.

Of domestic architecture in the Middle Ages the best and most widely distributed was monastic, and it must have set an important standard in its day. But since in France there was no Dissolution of the monasteries as in England, subsequent rebuilding has in most instances removed all traces of medieval structures, which have been replaced by those of the seventeenth and eighteenth centuries. Nevertheless, there are some interesting exceptions to this rule, including some early hospitals for the care of the sick, or

HÔTEL DE LA MONNAIE, FIGEAC

Maisons Dieu, as they were termed, which by the end of the Middle Ages had become numerous as an expression of the charity of the devout. The earliest seems to have been the Hôtel-Dieu in Paris, founded in the mid-seventh century and always associated with the cathedral.

The first purpose-built hospital accommodation of monastic origin tended to be, predictably, arranged round a cloister, on to which opened timber-galleried wards – rather like a sanatorium – with pharmacy, kitchens, and staff quarters. Large wards resembled churches, like the three-aisled hall of Saint-Jean at Angers (1170's) with its domical rib vaults. Tonnerre (1293), on the other hand, is splendidly roofed with an open king-post timber roof. Usually windows were high up to avoid draughts and a chapel was placed at one end, open and so visible from all the beds, in each of which it was common to nurse more than one patient.

In the Hôtel-Dieu at Beaune (1443) a good late medieval complex has survived more or less as it was. There is a timber arcaded ground floor to the court, a first floor gallery, a great ward for thirty beds along the wall, a very spacious chapel and a staircase turret in the corner of the court. Apart from its special function, with its high gabled roof with patterned tiles and barge-boarded dormers with finials, it gives a good impression of medieval domestic architecture at its best.

University colleges and schools too were first associated with the church and monastic establishments, and large ones were similarly grouped round a cloister court. Toulouse has the late medieval Collège Saint-Raymond (restored as a museum), and Orléans a two-aisled building, the Salle des Thèses, originally, a reading room. Unfortunately, unlike those of Oxford, the early colleges of the University of Paris have not survived, and in any case they never had halls of residence like the English universities, as students always lived in lodgings in the more usual continental manner.

The larger examples of medieval domestic architecture were of course the royal palaces or residences, evolving from military forms from the fourteenth century. Thus the donjon at Vincennes was rebuilt more spaciously and the houses of the nobles grouped within it, inside the curtain wall, as shown in the *Très Riches Heures* of the Duc de Berry. In the time of Phillippe IV (*d.* 1314) royal power grew at the expense of both church and nobles, and the Parlement de Paris became the chief law court in the land. Fragments of the old royal Palais de la Cité from early in the century are preserved in the Palais de Justice in Paris, while what was then outside the walls, the moated donjon of the Louvre, became at the behest of Charles V a group of buildings of com- fortable proportions arranged round a courtyard and linked by an external spiral staircase. The tiled floors, painted walls and ceilings, and substantial fireplaces were those of the palatial buildings of the period.

The living apartments, audience chambers, and chapels of the huge Palais des Papes at Avignon also date from the fourteenth century and are exceptionally dignified and spacious, notably those in the high Tour de la Garde-Robe with its fourteenth- century frescoes showing forest and garden scenes commissioned for the chamber of Clement VI. Since this was a palace used by two popes it is a double design arranged round two courtyards.

The substantial French town house known as the *hôtel* began in the fifteenth century as a courtyard house with an imposing street façade: an adaptation of the older courtyard plan to urban conditions. Such are the Late Gothic Hôtel de Bourgtheroulde,

Rouen (1486), and of the same time, the English Embassy at Dijon with its fine figure carving and turret stair, and the Hôtel de Cluny, Paris (1485) – now the Musée de Cluny – where above an arcade the chapel sports an oriel window rich in Flamboyant tracery and carved details.

The best of all, however, is probably the house of the merchant banker Jacques Cœur at Bourges (1443). It is Late Gothic in that there is nothing symmetrical about it, yet there is a clarity that is unmedieval. It has an irregular arcaded court and seven projecting towers or turrets containing newel stairs; the Great Hall, principal apartments, and chapels are all on the first floor. Also in Bourges and about half a century later is the Maison de la reine Blanche.

The sixteenth century continued the quadrangular type of late medieval hôtel, but Flamboyant decoration gave way to Renaissance in the neighbourhood of royal palaces in Touraine and Normandy, e.g. the Hôtel d'Alluye, Blois (1508), the House of Agnes Sorel, Orléans (1520), and the Hôtel Pincé, Angers (1523) where high dormered roofs and turrets are accompanied by rich 'classical' decoration. The fifteenth-century Maison d'Adam in the same town is a timber-framed house, tall, gabled, and covered with a diamond pattern of beams. It shows how the timber-framed house clung to earlier forms while the stone-built house was ready to adapt to new and fashionable styles. Toulouse has

JACQUES CŒUR'S HOUSE, BOURGES

an interesting sixteenth-century red brick group: the Hôtel de Pins early Renaissance, the Hôtel d'Assézat classic, the Hôtels du Vieux Raisin and de Bagis an incipient Baroque. External sculptural decoration was lavishly applied here in the sixteenth century, especially figures, such as those on the last two hôtels, the work of Nicolas Bachelier. Dijon has another much-decorated group associated with Hugues Sambin. In Paris a sixteenth-century example is the Hôtel Carnavalet; remodelled in the seventeenth century, it is now a museum. Minus its wings, it still retains an impressive entrance façade.

Smaller medieval stone houses are widely distributed though not plentiful. Twelfth- and thirteenth-century examples may be dated from the type of window: round-headed Romanesque like those of the twelfth century at Cluny, pointed or depressed Gothic arches – though the straight lintel is also found. The thirteenth century saw the stone transome introduced, the next century the mullion. Examples are the hôtel de ville at Saint-Antonin (Tarn-et-Garonne), twelfth-century – since hôtels de ville were in the first place, as we have seen, just larger houses taken over – the Four du Chapitre, Rouen, thirteenth century, several at Cordes of the fourteenth century, and the early fifteenth-century house in the rue Montmorency, Paris known as the house of Nicolas Flamel. From the same time dates the tiny but substantially-built house at La Devinière, near Chinon, where the incomparable Rabelais was born, with its original fireplace and outside stairs.

Despite the use of stone for the houses of the better-off in districts where it was available, timber-framed houses were the most usual and many remain dating back to the sixteenth or even the fifteenth century. The technique was of course essentially Gothic. A strong oak structure on a stone or brick lower storey or footing was filled in with wall panels composed of 'wattle and daub', like the English 'Tudor' house. Its several storeys jettied out over the narrow streets and its tall pointed gables gave a picturesque appearance, if one remote from classical canons. The ground floor was occupied by the workroom or shop, the first floor by the living rooms, and the second (and third, if any) by bedrooms. Behind the house was a court with a spiral staircase and sometimes a gallery linking it to another building across the court.

The house at 3 rue Volta, Paris, dates from the fourteenth century. Early examples are plainer than later ones with carved barge boards such as the more embellished house of Diane de Poitiers, Rouen (1525), where the abundant ornament is Early Renaissance in style. Normandy had, until the savage fighting at the Liberation, many good timber-framed houses at Rouen, Caen, and Lisieux; and there are those at Vitré in Brittany, Beauvais, Chartres, Strasbourg and small towns like Riquewihr and Kochersberg in Alsace, and Albi in the south. Timber-frame construction was also well used in the construction of farm buildings and for market halls.

More restricted by geographical and cultural conditions than by such factors as fashion, the vernacular architecture of the regions carries on medieval forms into later centuries. Thus the tall-roofed often timber-framed houses of Burgundy, e.g. those at Autun, bearing a family likeness to those of south Germany and the upper Rhineland, are obviously the descendants of Gothic structures. Some, however, are built of beautiful yellow local stone, as at the tiny feudal village of Brancion with its castle, covered market, and diminutive Romanesque village church, such a contrast to the former vastness of Cluny not many miles away. In Brittany large random rubble walls of granite rock have a distinctive character (as befits a region which has preserved

PONT SAINT-BÉNÉZET, AVIGNON

its own language and culture) and, as it were, rugged Celtic affinities with Cornwall across the Channel. There are many old houses in towns like Morlaix and Tréguier. On the Dordogne, Argentat has quaint and picturesque examples.

There is not space available in this short history to go into the rural vernacular of France, which is a large subject in itself. Suffice it to say that the historical factor is less important than local building traditions, which to a large extent are a response to geographical conditions – geology, climate, availability of timber, farming systems, etc. It is this adaptation which often makes surprisingly satisfying architecture out of the humble work of anonymous craftsmen rather than trained architects.

In addition to Brittany, Picardy, Lorraine, the Loire region, Provence, and the Pyrenees all possess distinctive local types; though the nineteenth century with its cheap rail transport began a trend towards increasing uniformity which no doubt will grow stronger with the dissemination of industrial materials and the more widespread adoption of the idioms of modern architecture.

Perhaps the most famous of all French medieval bridges is the late twelfth century Pont d'Avignon (Pont St-Bénézet), with its

PONT VALENTRÉ, CAHORS

chapel half-way across, as was occasionally the custom to dispose it. This was a work of the Frères Pontifs or gild of bridge builders. Another fine romantic specimen of a later date is the fortified Valentré bridge at Cahors with its tall pyramidal capped towers through which the causeway passes, high over the River Lot.

CHAPTER FIVE

Early Renaissance

THE first Renaissance building in France is the small chapel in the old cathedral of Saint-Lazare at Marseille (1475) by Francesco Laurana, a sculptor working for the art-loving René, Duke of Anjou and Provence. But not until the invasion of Italy by Charles VIII in 1494 did contact with Renaissance architecture really develop, three-quarters of a century after it began in Italy.

Much admired in Louis XII's time and a source of great influence in France was the decoration of the Certosa, the famous Carthusian monastery outside Pavia, actually nearer to Flamboyant in its rich fantasy than to the spirit of the High Renaissance. Hence, perhaps, its appeal to the French.

To begin with, the Renaissance spirit was seen in funerary monuments, often by Italians, such as the ornament of the Flamboyant Easter Sepulchre at Solesmes (1496), and in fittings like the screen in the abbey church of Fécamp (1519). But at the Château de Gaillon, Normandy (1508), built for the great Cardinal d'Amboise, superimposed orders of classical pilasters were first applied systematically to a French Gothic building.

This was to prove characteristic of Early Renaissance architecture in France: classical – especially Lombard – motifs and detail, sometimes inaccurate, being added by way of fashionable ornament to an essentially late medieval carcass. In spite of the pilasters this would retain its rib-vaulted great hall (smaller ones were covered with coffered timber ceilings) with Gothic windows, and its high pitched roofs elaborately varied in a picturesque medieval manner. Gothic verticality is still strongly marked, but a new symmetry begins to be noticeable in planning and in the composition of elevations with regularly disposed superimposed windows and a separate order allotted to each storey, strengthening the horizontal lines of the building.

There is a new opening up of the façades by means of loggias, though the climate of France did not encourage their extensive use as in Italian Renaissance architecture. It did however encourage larger mullioned and transomed windows to admit more light and the use of tall chimneys which became characteristic features, decorative as well as functional.

The principal growing point of the Early Renaissance in France was the brilliant court of François I who like his predecessors, Charles VIII and Louis XII, had direct contact with Italian culture during his sojourn in Italy. The French were fascinated by Italy at this time, impressed by its luxurious living and works of art, and it was in conscious imitation of the Italian courts that François I – in one way 'the last product of chivalry; in another the first modern King of France' – shaped his.

It was visited by Lucca della Robbia, Andrea del Sarto, Serlio and Primaticcio, while the great Leonardo spent his last years there, dying in 1519. They were artists and designers who for the most part relied in their architectural work on French masons and craftsmen to carry their ideas into effect and therefore had to adapt them to still flourishing medieval techniques and the lack of a classical tradition, to say nothing of a climate, already referred to, wetter and colder than most of Italy.

But the French were soon to evolve their individual version of the Renaissance style. Like Elizabethan architecture in England, it is occasionally barbarous or clumsy by Italian standards but has remarkable vigour and imagination of its own.

Already there were plenty of medieval churches and, as in Tudor England, the swing from ecclesiastical to domestic building is very

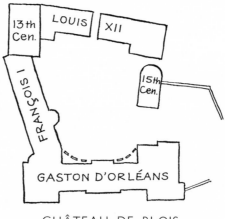

CHÂTEAU DE BLOIS

marked. Most of the major works of the earlier part of the sixteenth century are situated in what was the much favoured hunting
country of the Val de Loire, châteaux or country houses first
constructed of brick and stone in Louis xii's time and then all in
stone, a rather friable calcareous variety.

The Château of Blois has parts dating from the thirteenth
century (the Tour de Foix, the gateway to the court, and the Salle
des États) to the seventeenth century, all ranged round an irregular
quadrangle. But to this period belongs the eastern or François i
wing (1498–1515).

The façades have large windows with panelled, not moulded,
mullions, superimposed pilasters – as at Gaillon – prominent
cornices and ornamental dormer windows and chimney stacks.
The latter, with the high roofs with which they are associated,
are highly characteristic of Early French Renaissance and are
obviously quite unlike anything out of Renaissance Italy. The
general irregularity of Blois is Gothic, not Renaissance, as is the
richly carved wood panelling in the interior.

The medieval newel staircase of Louis xii was in part the model

STAIRCASES: BLOIS AND CHAMBORD

CHÂTEAU DE CHENONCEAUX

for the famous open staircase tower of François I in the courtyard, but this evidently owed something to designs for staircases by Leonardo. The classical detailing applied to it is rather alien to the general lines of what is essentially a Gothic form and structure, spiralling upwards. But the spatial quality and monumentality are new. It shows Bramantesque influence, but is mostly north Italian with some heraldic ornament, a characteristic Early Renaissance mixture.

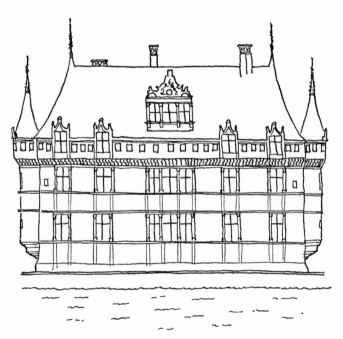

CHÂTEAU D'AZAY-LE-RIDEAU

The seventeenth-century work at Blois, by François Mansart – not the inventor of the roomy and typically French Mansard roof, despite tradition – is in a much more restrained and correct form of classicism than the Early Renaissance work just described, but it also includes a square open newel staircase.

The Château of Chenonceaux (1515) and the Château d'Azay-le-Rideau (1518), on the other hand, both have as an innovation replacing the earlier spiral type of staircase, two straight parallel flights of steps. Chenonceaux is also interesting for its elaborately ornamented doors, Flamboyant motifs, and plain but picturesque bridge gallery (1556) later built over the River Cher by Delorme for its famous owner, Diane de Poitiers, the powerful mistress of Henri II. An interesting contrast in style may be observed between these two phases as will be explained later in this chapter.

These two châteaux are among the smaller ones built for rich and successful *bourgeois* clients and are noticeably regular in design – the Chenonceaux of this period being a square with corner towers. At both the architecture is complemented by the presence of water that reflects it and enhances its poetic qualities. The combination seems universally irresistible in architecture and there have always been architects ready to exploit such effects.

At the superb royal Château of Chambord (1519), a new building designed by the Italian, Domenico da Cortona, and executed by Pierre Nepveu, who probably worked on other Loire châteaux, Renaissance axial planning may be unmistakably observed for perhaps the first time in France, despite the basically medieval conception of a keep with round towers. The interior is the first

CHÂTEAU DE CHAMBORD

example of an ordered arrangement of rooms in contrast to the irregular, almost haphazard medieval interior planning.

In Cortona's design appears also for the first time the *appartement* or group of rooms as a unit of domestic planning; it was to become very fashionable in France, a standard arrangement. There is a splendid double spiral staircase of a type Leonardo was interested in, though there had been medieval examples of the double spiral type already in France. The staircase is placed at the centre of the main block and from it on each floor extend four elliptically barrel-vaulted corridors with *appartements* in each corner. Externally, it is marked with a storeyed lantern.

The exterior of Chambord itself, despite the debased classical pilasters – the capitals are unique – shell-headed niches, colonnettes, and other Renaissance detail, and despite the horizontal emphasis of cornices and string courses, is still that of a French Gothic building. It has large mullioned windows and from its terraced roof rise high-pitched, extravagantly developed gabled roofs with elaborate dormers, lofty chimneys (already noted at Blois), and large round angle towers with domes and conical roof. Large circular towers and turrets with conical roofs were of course a feature of late medieval castles and persisted well into the sixteenth century in the Early Renaissance châteaux, as well as influencing the architecture of Scotland through the 'Auld Alliance'.

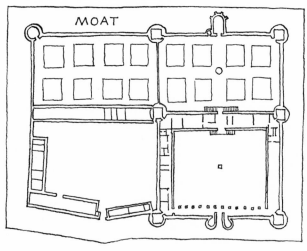

CHÂTEAU DE BURY

There is a good deal of interesting small detail, such as un-classical-looking pilasters applied to door frames and to dormer windows and characteristic mouldings of the period which evolved from both medieval and classical sources.

A few miles from Blois but now in ruins is the Château de Bury (1520), once typical of its period. The main block or *corps de logis* was of three storeys and had terminal towers; the side wings which accommodated services and stabling were of two storeys; while the fourth side of the quadrangular court consisted of a one-storey screen wall with a towered central entrance with porte-cochère and an internal arcade ending in a round tower at each end. On the opposite side of the château was the garden – a pleasance of the Italian type now becomes a part of the total design – with a chapel placed on the central axis on the far side. This was the type of plan which was to reappear time and again in the châteaux and hotels or large town houses of France. (It was first used for the latter by Serlio in La Grand Ferrare, 1544.)

Elevational treatment resembles Chenonceaux and Azay in its flatness and rectilinear character produced by string courses and pilasters. Dormers are also much in evidence.

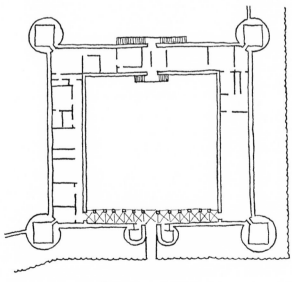

CHÂTEAU DE BURY

CHÂTEAU DE SULLY

Among the fortress-type Loire châteaux, Gothic with Renaissance interiors, are Fougères (1470), Langeais, and Loches; both the latter also having their early medieval donjons. The magnificent Chaumont, already mentioned, has a proud castellated exterior with a fine Renaissance interior. Clearly it is a transitional work with later additions. The Château de Valençay, which now houses the splendid Talleyrand collection, was begun in the mid-sixteenth century in the Early Renaissance style of Chambord but continued building for over two hundred years. There is grand Baroque work in the court and a new tower was added towards the end of the eighteenth century; the effect is rich and picturesque. The Château de Sully, acquired by Henri IV's powerful minister, belongs to the same Loire group, and so does Montrésor not far from Loches.

La Rochefoucauld (1525), near Angoulême, is a very unified and quite successful example of an Italianate château of the period.

The Château de Saint-Germain-en-Laye (1539), probably by Pierre Chambiges, is another, much restored, Early Renaissance building (now the Musée d'Antiquités Nationales) where the transition between late Gothic and classical may be studied. The plan kept to the original castle but to the court were built richly arcaded classical stone façades with brick decoration and cupolaed

CHÂTEAU DE MONTRÉSOR

staircase turrets. A notable innovation is the Renaissance flat roof – resting on Gothic vaulting – with its balustrade and vases. Of the later additions to Saint-Germain the best is perhaps Le Nôtre's magnificent terrace two and a half kilometres long overlooking the Seine.

SAINT-GERMAIN-EN-LAYE, THE COURT

Saint-Germain belongs mainly, however, to the period after the late 1520's when François 1 left the Loire for the Paris region which, since it attracted the nobility, thus became the second centre of French Renaissance architecture. Towards the end of François 1's reign the Château de Madrid was built in the Bois de Boulogne: two high squares with corner turrets connected by a hall opened up on both sides by loggias, a motif deriving from the Italian villa. Unfortunately it only survives in Du Cerceau's engravings, though its rich Mannerist decoration, much of it terra cotta, was an important source for later architects. Italian Renaissance influence increases in this later group of châteaux, though they are less intrinsically interesting than the Loire group.

Perhaps the best known is Gilles le Breton's remodelling of a medieval castle for François 1 as the Palais de Fontainebleau, begun in the same year as the Madrid works, 1528. This is a very large conception by the son of the clerk-of-works at Chambord – High Renaissance in derivation – where despite the irregularity due to later extensions by the Italians Vignola and Serlio there is a fresh simplicity and new important motifs. Such are the Porte Dorée with its three large arched superimposed recesses, a clever reshaping of the six storey medieval structure by putting two tiers of windows into each of the three storeys of the new classical

FONTAINEBLEAU, PORTE DORÉE

FONTAINEBLEAU

design; the pedimented windows which flank it; the spacious outside staircase with its two curved arms towards the Cour du Cheval Blanc; and, formerly, an external staircase inside the Cour Ovale, also with two arms and leading to the frontispiece with detached columns, features associated with mid-sixteenth-century work.

The staircases, originating in the late fourteenth century Vis du Louvre, Paris, were the culmination of the medieval newel type, and the exterior is dominated by the high French roofs and dormers, but much more within the control of a classical discipline than had been so hitherto. The north side of the Cour du Cheval Blanc is the most important piece of Renaissance design in it, despite the absence of strict symmetry in fenestration.

There is fine new style interior decoration by the Italians Primaticcio and Rosso. It is Mannerist, in the latest style: painting and stucco in the tradition of Raphael's interiors plus northern wood-carving. It is in these sumptuous sixteenth-century fashion-ably Mannerist saloons – the Galerie de François I (1532) and the Galerie de Henri II – and in its general lay-out of courts and formal gardens which makes Fontainebleau attractive, rather than its exterior façades which are less successful than those of other early châteaux.

Altogether, however, it is a key building in the evolution of classical design in France. In it Le Breton seems to have created the particularly French versions of Renaissance architecture; it

FONTAINEBLEAU

was followed and perfected in the Aile de la Belle Cheminée (1568) by Primaticcio. This is a somewhat dry, cold kind of classicism and not what might have been expected from his earlier Mannerist work. But as we shall soon see, French architecture had by this time undergone an important development. Rather earlier are the châteaux of Villandry (1532) and Champigny-sur-Veude, both in the Loire valley. They are clearly of the same family as Le Breton's Fontainebleau, with older touches in the fretted dormers of Villandry. The early seventeenth-century formal gardens at Villandry, where even the kitchen garden is divided into hedged enclosures, is a superb example of the art as it was before Le Nôtre arrived on the scene.

In the Île de France, Villers-Cotterets, a charming product of the 1530's and more modest in scale than most, has the King's Lodging of François I. Situated between two courts, it is Italianate early French Renaissance work under the influence of the gateway of the Court Ovale at Fontainebleau and was the work of members of Le Breton's family. The decoration is distinctly Mannerist.

The chapel at Champigny has a fine barrel-vaulted porch (1570) and is a product of a later phase of French Renaissance architecture now to be considered.

The third stage in the evolution of the French Renaissance style coincides with the emergence of several notable French architects who had gone to Rome to study in the 1530's; the arrival of Sebastiano Serlio as *architecteur du roi* in 1540; and, later on, Primaticcio's work at Fontainebleau just referred to. This is the step from Early to High Renaissance. To deal with Serlio's contribution first: a former pupil of Palladio, he built the Hôtel

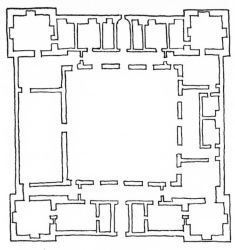

CHÂTEAU D'ANCY-LE-FRANC

d'Este (1546) and perhaps the Hôtel Montpensier, both at Fontainebleau though only the gateways remain, and he was responsible for the fine classical Château d'Ancy-le-Franc (1546) near Tonnerre, quadrangular in plan with square towers at the corners. The Italianate façade, rusticated on the ground floor, has pilasters as already applied, but in the courtyard elevation Serlio used double pilasters with niches between at each main bay, a sort of triumphal arch motif which Bramante had used in the Cortile di Belvedere at the Vatican. This was to be taken up (together with a design by Serlio for the rebuilding of the palace) by the

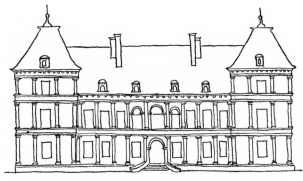

CHÂTEAU D'ANCY-LE-FRANC

new French architects, as in Pierre Lescot's inner façade of the new Palais du Louvre, on the site of the medieval castle, where it emphasizes the main ascents.

Lescot was a scholar and friend of François 1 and Ronsard. His work is in the south-west corner of the square court, the western part dating from 1546, the southern from 1578. The façades, consisting of two storeys and an attic, now replacing dormer windows, are symmetrical with superimposed orders of decorative Corinthian and Composite pilasters and regularly spaced windows with alternating triangular and segmental pediments. Prominent features are the projecting pavilions, varied fenestration, vertical emphases in the façades, and generally ornamental character of the design. The great pitched roof is also typically French. The flat oval shields with hanging garlands, the segmental pediments, and the plentiful use of refined sculptural decoration by the sculptor Jean Goujon in the upper parts of the design are already French classic and quite distinct from anything in contemporary Italy.

Goujon also collaborated with Lescot – trained as a painter – at the Hôtel Carnavalet (c. 1544), remodelled a hundred years later by François Mansart, and on the exquisite Fontaine des Innocents (1547), both in Paris. Their style is less monumental than Italian Renaissance and, as one might expect from two such men, an essentially decorative one.

The basis of this new mid-sixteenth-century mode is classical

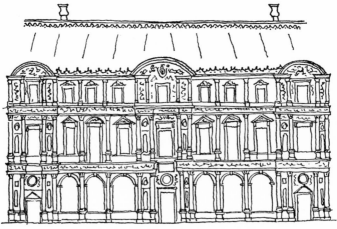

LOUVRE, SQUARE COURT

orders, now known more correctly through the treatises of Vitruvius and the theorists of the Italian Renaissance architecture, either superimposed (usually Doric, Ionic, and Corinthian on top) or in giant orders running up the height of the façade. The high-pitched Gothic roof *à la française* was still preferred to the flat Italian type but domes were also brought in.

Serlio's famous and highly influential treatise *Architettura* came out in 1537, the later books, like his building work, showing increasing French influence the longer he remained north of the Alps. But these new French scholar architects also wrote treatises. The first widely read French translation of the Roman architect Vitruvius was Jean Martin's of 1546. Jean Bullant's *Reigle générale d'Architecture* on the Orders appeared in 1564, Philibert Delorme's *Nouvelles Inventions* in 1561 and his *Traité d'Architecture* in 1567 – an original contribution to architectural theory which, though deriving from native medieval tradition, again marked an advance on that of the Renaissance.

Delorme more than any before him combined engineering skill with an impressive body of classical learning. He was in no sense a copyist of Italian Renaissance architects but possessed a talent which put him on a par with them. In his sense of rationality, despite his classical education, he is like his contemporary in literature, Ronsard. This is the time when a French classicism is discernible in architecture as in the work of the Pléiade.

Among the most famous of the works of this period are Jacques Ancrouet Du Cerceau's engravings of *Les plus excellents Bâtiments de France* (1576).

All these helped enormously to disseminate the Renaissance style in France, and in England too. But it was still chiefly a matter of elements and something of the spirit, freely and experimentally used, compared with the more wholehearted classicism yet to come.

Philibert Delorme was one of the first French architects to study in Rome, inventive, original, and a friend of Rabelais. Regrettably, despite his importance, no complete building by his hand has survived. He used the triumphal arch motif for the fine frontispiece of the grand Château d'Anet (1547) built for Diane de Poitiers; it is now in the court of the École des Beaux-Arts with the earlier portico from Gaillon. The two works illustrate well the difference between the Early and High Renaissance style in French architecture. The Anet work has three orders, one above the

CHÂTEAU D'ANET, ENTRANCE

other: Tuscan Doric, Ionic, Corinthian – and again French sculptural decoration. It has a classical correctness and monumental grandeur unprecedented in French architecture and was to prove a most influential design.

So was the plan which became a standard one for over a hundred years: three ranges round a quadrangular court with a fourth lower entrance range. The entrance gate (*c.* 1552) still stands. Quite unique, it illustrates perfectly Delorme's ability to produce a monumental design without imitating the Italian High Renaissance. The small French Renaissance chapel at Anet (*c.* 1560), a memorial to Diane de Poitiers, may be by Bullant. Centralized and domed, it was the first ecclesiastical building in that style but was too novel to produce followers in its day.

Delorme was the first to invent a specifically 'French' order with rusticated columns with bands of ornament – a motif soon to be used by de Brosse at the Palais de Luxembourg, Paris – and it was he who introduced the dome.

Jean Bullant too, *architecte du Roi*, had studied in Rome and used the triumphal arch motif similarly to Delorme at his remodelling of the Château d'Écouen (1545) for the Duc de Montmorency, his first important job. But in another design at the same place he introduced the giant orders (used unclassically), first employed

CHÂTEAU D'ANET, THE CHAPEL

by Michelangelo only a little before in the palaces on the Capitoline Hill, to support his richly carved entablature. The use of these colossal columns became very popular in France.

About the same time Bullant also worked for Montmorency at the Châtelet at Chantilly (*c.* 1560). The notable feature here is the sophisticated Mannerist syncopation of the façades produced by the large order cutting across the division into two storeys. Though Bullant's early style is somewhat stiltedly 'correct', based on that of Delorme, he later tended to a Mannerist fantasy similar to Du Cerceau, as at Chantilly, part of the forecourt and gallery over the bridge at Chenonceaux (*c.* 1576) and the bridge and gallery at Fère-en-Tardenois (1552), now in a ruinous state, which makes allusion to the Roman viaducts.

Aside from the Châtelet of Bullant, Chantilly, now a magnificent gallery and museum, was begun in the time of François I in the Italianate early Renaissance style of the Loire château, and later, in the seventeenth century, rebuilt by Mansart for the great Prince de Condé when Le Nôtre laid out the gardens and park. But perhaps the most impressive conception at Chantilly are the Great Stables (1719) for the regal state of the Duc de Bourbon. Never can horses have been housed so sumptuously, though this was by no means a unique essay in palatial riding school and stable building (see p. 137).

In 1564 Delorme and Bullant began work on the Palais des Tuileries for Catherine de Médicis. The finest work of the second half of the sixteenth century, this was the residence of French monarchs until it was savagely destroyed by the Commune in 1871. A complex arranged on multiple axes round five courts on the lines of the Escorial in Madrid, the main square at the centre was flanked by rectangular ones on either side with high pavilions at the entrance and at the corners of the courts.

Delorme also built the Château of St. Maur-des-Fossés (c. 1540) when he returned from Rome, and the design for François I's tomb at St Denis is also his. St Maur is a single-storey building reminiscent of the Palazzo del Tè by Giulio Romano but is French in its corner pavilions and mullioned windows. It was the first essay in decorating an entire building with one order of pilasters disposed in the High Renaissance manner, one more instance of Delorme's grasp of the true classic manner. Yet neither Delorme or Bullant really understood the spirit of the Italian Renaissance if judged by the standards of later architects, despite their early and first-hand contact with it in Rome; that is if they ever really wanted to, for first and foremost they were Frenchmen.

Catharine de Médicis continued Lescot's work at the Louvre along the south or river side, and to it the Tuileries was joined by Du Cerceau's two galleries. Plainer than the Louvre, it relied more on its proportions for effect. In the centre (1565) Delorme used the first dome in Paris and superimposed orders, Doric and Corinthian, beside his own original ringed French order already referred to, fragments of which may be inspected in the present Jardins des Tuileries on the former site of the palace. The pavilions had giant orders characteristic of Bullant. Completion of the Tuileries was the work of Le Vau and D'Orbay (1680).

Interesting work in the south-west of France about the middle of the sixteenth century is associated with Guillaume Philander who added a 'Roman' gable to the façade of Rodez cathedral in

9. St-Eustache, Paris (1532): the high rib-vaulted nave of Delorme's essentially Gothic design magnificently translated into Early Renaissance terms with pilastered piers and an arcade of classical arches. The west front is eighteenth century.

10*a*. Palais de Fontainebleau: the early sixteenth-century Galerie de François 1er. A sumptuous interior of carved woodwork, painting, and stucco in the transalpine Mannerist style of the court school fertilised by imported Italian ideas

10*b*. Château de Blois: the François 1er wing (*c.* 1500) has an Early Renaissance façade with superimposed orders and ornamental chimneys. The high roof and oriel windows are a Gothic inheritance. Compare F. Mansart's classicism to the right.

1562. His east gallery at the Château de Bournazel, Aveyron (c. 1550) shows the sort of correct monumental classicism of Delorme, but with regional differences, nevertheless. Philander was a pupil of Serlio and, like other architects of the period, a writer, who published a translation of Vitruvius in 1543.

Ideas of Renaissance classical planning such as the Tuileries exemplified were propagated by the designer and founder of an architectural dynasty, already mentioned for his book: Jacques Androuet Du Cerceau, who also studied in Rome in the thirties. But his Château Verneuil-sur-Oise (1565) reverted to the simpler quadrangular tradition of Anet, a much less classic mixture. This was a late work, as was his Château of Charleval (1572), of which little remains. Both were characteristically over-ornamented with much fantastic detail and had French pavilion roofs. He was more a decorator and designer than an architect, as both his buildings and his engravings evince. La Tour d'Aigues (1560) is an adaptation of the Pavillon du Roi of Lescot's Louvre, but the later main entrance is much more reminiscent of a Roman triumphal arch, despite its French use of an unbroken entablature over free-standing columns. Not surprisingly, it is in Provence. Few other great country houses were built at this time because of the internal disorders and Wars of Religion between Catholics and Protestants lasting from the death of Henry II in 1559 until Henri IV found Paris 'worth a mass' in 1589, thirty years later. What building there was showed a falling away from the more consistent classicism which had developed and a reversion to a more hybrid style.

Notable hôtels de ville of the later sixteenth century were those of Paris – still being built, though begun by François I, and the first Early Renaissance building in Paris, regrettably destroyed in the Commune of 1871 – and that of La Rochelle (1597) one of the outstanding secular buildings of the reign of Henri IV, in a somewhat ponderous Mannerist style. Tesson's wing at Arras (1572) shows the same agitated qualities already noted in the work of Du Cerceau the Elder. There is probably Flemish influence here as in the Halle Échevinale at Lille (1593) by Fayet.

Of schools and colleges of the Early Renaissance there is nothing before those which Henri IV allowed the Counter-Reformation order of the Society of Jesus to build. Many of them were desigated by Père Étienne Martellange and are still used as lycées in most instances. They are generally planned round several courts, for

I

example those of the masters, the classrooms, and the boarding accommodation at La Flêche, where the youthful Descartes studied. Other examples are the Lycée Henri IV in the abbey of Sainte-Geneviève, Paris, and the Lycée Malherbe at Caen in the old Abbaye-aux-Hommes.

Before turning once more to French ecclesiastical architecture to observe what innovations the Renaissance had brought, there are two more important secular works by the Huguenot architect Salomon de Brosse which should be noted: the Palais du Luxembourg, Paris (1615) – now the Senate House – and the Palais de Justice, Rennes (1618), his last major work.

The first was built for Marie de Médicis, Henri II's widow, in the bold simple Florentine Renaissance style with Mannerist

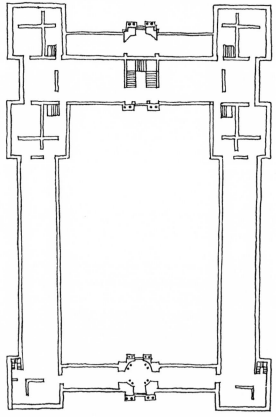

PALAIS DU LUXEMBOURG

PALAIS DU LUXEMBOURG

motifs from the Palazzo Pitti, e.g. rustication, except that the high roofs and tall chimney stacks are of course French. So are the independently roofed pavilions which, as at Fontainebleau and the Louvre, emphasize the centre and terminations of the façades. The plan is also of a type already characterized as French, being in the Anet tradition. It consists of a three-storey corps de logis, two-storey side wings, and a single-storey screen range along the fourth side of the court. There is a porte-cochère. The late sixteenth century had brought in the vogue for the formal, geometrically planned Italian garden related to the house, e.g. Charleval and Saint Germain en Laye (where it was terraced like the Villa d'Este) and the gardens at the Luxembourg are of this type. Thus it is a typical great *hôtel*, and the climax of this particular phase of French architectural development as it remains to us. Above all, de Brosse was the first French architect since Delorme to conceive buildings in terms of mass rather than decorated surfaces as the Du Cerceaux did.

At Rennes over a rusticated ground floor the first-floor façade is articulated with a widely spaced rhythm of pilasters and coupled pilasters, and the steep roof is unbroken by raised pavilions. It is

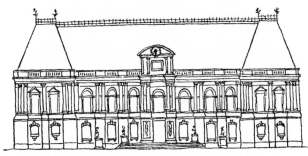

PALAIS DE JUSTICE, RENNES

a very French design, but its Palladianism hints of French classic to come, even anticipating the work of François Mansart.

De Brosse's work also included the Aqueduct of Arcueil, the châteaux of Coulommiers and Blérancourt, and the Hôtel de Liancourt, Paris, all about 1616. Blérancourt shows an interesting departure as well as De Brosse's sense of mass. It consists of a *corps de logis* with flanking square-domed pavilions but no wings or court. The compactness is new and points forward again to F. Mansart, as well as looking over its shoulder to the Italian Renaissance.

In his ecclesiastical designs de Brosse produced tall, rather crowded, be-columned classical façades, like that of Saint-Gervais (1616). Based on Delorme's frontispiece at Anet, this is a French equivalent of contemporary Roman church façades.

But for churches the Gothic style of architecture had never quite died out. Thus Orléans Cathedral was built in it from the time of Henri IV to that of Louis XVI; and the nineteenth century, with its neo-Gothic towers, was to bring a return to it. In the early sixteenth century Renaissance motifs in church architecture appear first, as was said earlier on, in fittings and monuments. Among these are the outstanding tombs of Louis XII (1515) in the Abbey of Saint-Denis and of the Cardinals of Amboise in Rouen Cathedral (1522). Architecturally employed, the new manner was applied superficially to what was essentially a late Gothic

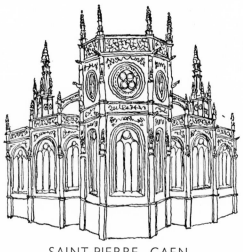

SAINT-PIERRE, CAEN

structure by Hector Sohier in his richly decorated apsidal chapels for the fourteenth-century church of Saint-Pierre, Caen, and in a more purely Italian form in the Valois Chapel (1560) at Saint-Denis by Primaticcio. The latter was round, centrally planned with six radiating chapels and internal columns in two orders arranged in the Bramantesque manner. Its dome was notable as being the first in France.

Of churches proper the most significant designs are those of Saint-Étienne-du-Mont (1517) and Saint-Eustache (1532), both in Paris; they show an amalgam of very fine Gothic structure and superficial Renaissance elements.

The first is planned like a medieval church with the nave arcade fitted with 'Doric' capitals supporting rib vaulting and there is an unusual ambulatory above it. Across the nave is the celebrated *jubé* or rood screen (*c.* 1545) by Delorme with its double spiral staircases and ornate pierced Renaissance balustrades. The centre of the steeply gabled façade (1620) has a doorway with an architectural frame of composite columns supporting an entablature and sculptured pediment. Above, set in a segmental pediment, is a circular window with 'Gothic' tracery, and beyond rises a lofty tower with cupola.

Saint-Eustache by Delorme and Dominico da Cortona, the Frenchified Italian architect of the hôtel de ville, is similarly arranged on medieval lines – High Gothic rather than Flamboyant – with double aisles, apse, round-headed traceried windows, high roof, and flying buttresses. To this is added Renaissance ornamental detail such as pilasters on walls and buttresses. It was not

WINDOW TRACERY, SAINT-EUSTACHE, PARIS

completed until 1654, and the façade of two towers with recessed portals is actually as late as 1772.

Saint-Nicolas-des-Champs, Paris (1575), has a 'triumphal arch' side porch, a motif which had appeared earlier in the façade of Saint-Nizier, Troyes (1535), one of several Flamboyant churches in that town with classical touches: columns, pilasters, pediments, round-headed openings, screens, etc. The church of Montrésor and the chapel of Ussé are examples from Touraine. Dijon has the façade of Saint-Michel (1537) as well as the interesting sculptured front of the Maison Milsand (c. 1561) by Hugues Sambin. Sixteenth-century piers become square in section and sometimes columns have attached pilasters.

The principles of Renaissance town planning were first formulated in Italy in the sixteenth century, though prosperous cities there and in the Low Countries had enjoyed the convenience of a central market place or square since the latter part of the Middle Ages. They were principles which went back to the days of Imperial Rome and were to be revived again at Pienza and especially in Sistine Rome. But they were to be perfected chiefly in France where the finest squares of the seventeenth and eighteenth centuries were designed. As we have seen, a rectilinear lay-out was adopted in the bastide towns of the south-west, undoubtedly on Roman precedent, but the Renaissance came to appreciate the straight line, geometrical shapes, and unity not just for its usefulness in laying out and developing a district but as a matter of rational principle and aesthetic choice.

Systematically planned French towns of the sixteenth and seventeenth centuries showing the implementation of Renaissance ideas are Vitry-le-François, Charleville and Henrichemont. The finest is undoubtedly Richelieu, founded by the Cardinal of that name in 1631, consideration of which is deferred until the next chapter.

When after a period of internecine strife Henri IV acquired Paris he attempted to provide housing for the bourgeoisie, which he and his minister Sully fostered as a bulwark against the aristocracy, a population now growing in size and importance, by laying out a number of residential squares that were to be followed all over Europe in the years ahead.

In France, then, Renaissance town planning begins with Henri IV's Place Royale (1605), now the Place des Vosges. Inspired by the Piazza at Leghorn, it is a rectangular 'square' surrounded by uniform façades of prosperous town houses in a Dutch-derived domestic style so that a second source is clearly evident. Brick was now frequently used at this period. The Dutch favoured the material, being short of good building stone, and it allowed construction to proceed quickly. Here stone dressings are used, including quoins and bands of stone, and ornament is rather heavy, continuing the Mannerist style of the last part of the sixteenth century. Ground floors are rusticated basements with shops, arcaded to providing sheltered walls, and the two storeys above are finished with high roofs and dormers. The result was a mode which was popular from this time until about the 1630's (see the Châteaux of Grosbois, resembling Henri IV's Stable Court at Fontainebleau by Rémy Collin, and Rosny-sur-Seine (c. 1600); and the more restlessly Late Mannerist Château de Brissac near Angers, more typical of the elaboration favoured in the provinces).

Originally only one corner of the square was open and the main entrance was through the taller and more elaborate Pavillons du Roi et de la Reine in the middle of the blocks. Essentially such plans were introverted from the urban bustle about them to provide residential districts both dignified and tranquil.

The Place Dauphine (1606) illustrates another type of central-ized plan, for it was a triangular 'square' occupying the tip of the

PLACE DES VOSGES

Île de la Cité, pointing to a statue of Henri IV at the entrance of the Pont-Neuf, the 'new bridge' – actually the oldest in Paris. This was built by Baptiste Du Cerceau, son of J. A. Du Cerceau, and probably the architect of the Hôtel d'Angoulême, afterwards called the Hôtel Lamoignon (1584), a design with a colossal order of pilasters recalling Bullant rather than his father's style. Though only two of the houses retain their original appearance and the triangle has been broken in to by the late nineteenth-century Palais de Justice, it too was once uniform and surrounded by housing of the type in the Place des Vosges just described. These were the first of the famous *places royales* of monumental town planning in France; though the royal statues which provided them with a focal point have long since been banished. French provincial examples include the squares at Charleville (1608), Montauban, and Richelieu; and outside France, Covent Garden (*c.* 1630) – the ancestor of all the later English developments.

CHAPTER SIX

The Seventeenth Century

FEW churches were built in France during the second half of the sixteenth century on account of the Wars of Religion, a period of dislocation lasting from Henri II's death (1559) to the Edict of Nantes (1598) which permitted freedom of worship to the Protestants.

With the spread of the Society of Jesus in France in the early seventeenth century the number of large preaching churches required by this order increased and the period saw the adoption of the Jesuit plan and façade invented by Vignola in the Gesù, Rome. Thus the Chapel of the Jesuit College, La Flèche, a work by Le Père Martellange, has a nave with side-chapels executed in an Early Renaissance style, while the earliest surviving example of a façade of the Gesù type is that of Saint-Gervais (1616) – possibly by de Brosse – and there are others too: Sainte-Élisabeth (1631) and Saint-Paul-Saint-Louis (1634). All three are in Paris.

Their façades are composed of coupled columns, pilasters, and pediments – an orthodox two-storey composition with volutes in the case of Sainte-Elisabeth; Saint-Gervais (1616) has a three-storey design of Doric, Ionic, and Corinthian orders, superimposed. This work, with which the name of de Brosse has been linked, and which echoes Lescot's Louvre despite its obvious debt to Roman Baroque, is a revolutionary one in that it introduces a third storey (because of the extra height of the church) on the pattern of the typical château frontispiece. Saint-Paul-Saint-Louis (1634) by Derand also has a three-tiered façade and is typical of the aisleless nave with side chapels already referred to. It is really an arrangement which goes back beyond Vignola to Alberti, but one cannot overlook the strong late medieval tradition in France of the internal buttress chapel as practised in the Languedoc under Catalan influence.

Plans in fact were generally more uniform than façades in these first classical churches to be built in France under Jesuit influence, particularly that of Le Père Martellange who had studied Vignola

SAINT-GERVAIS, PARIS

and to whom, with Le Père Derand, Saint-Paul-Saint-Louis is attributed. The dome is one of the earliest in Paris, and the florid decoration of the façade indicates the arrival of a Baroque manner from Italy. A French feature of the church, however, is the way the transepts project more than in Vignola's prototype plan. At Blois, Saint-Vincent-de-Paul by Martellange and Turnel is a similar church of the period.

On the other hand, the Jesuit churches at Bordeaux, Saint-Paul (1663), and Caen, Notre-Dame-de-la-Gloriette (1684), have the two-storey façade like the Gesù. Jesuit churches in France were more varied than is commonly acknowledged and included Gothic forms in northern France – such as the fine chapel of the Lycée Corneille, Rouen (1610), with its rib vaults and pointed Flamboyant windows – and in the Franche-Comté. La Flèche, too, retains 'Gothic' rib vaults.

The Jesuits were not a cloistered order, as is well-known, and their houses were therefore educational establishments and did not follow the conventional arrangement of the older orders.

Many other churches besides those of the Society of Jesus tended to follow their tradition in both plan and façade as at Notre-Dame, Le Havre (1605), with its ringed French order, and, somewhat clumsily, the Carthusian church of Saint-Bruno, Bordeaux (1611).

The fully classical Renaissance church did not appear until the seventeenth century, and it is to examples of this kind, typically domed and centralized, that we must now turn. First, the Sainte-Marie chapel of the Filles de la Visitation, Paris (1632), an early but mature work of François Mansart. It is a unified circular domed church with three domed oval main and side chapels on the major axes. The decoration is restrained and classical, consisting chiefly of flat panelling, but in places there survive rich Late Mannerist elements in the scrolls and *putti* heads. The interweaving spatial effects of the interior and the dramatic contrast in lighting between the darkened entrance and the light flooding down from the four lanterns of the domes show his mastery of Baroque design. Domes in fact became popular in Paris about this time, with classical groin and barrel vaults – the latter opened up to admit light at the sides – their appropriate complement instead of the medieval rib vault. Generally, however, because of her intellectual propensities, no doubt, France resisted the full implications of Baroque with its more extreme effects and tendency to

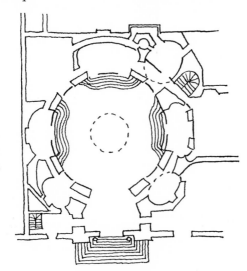

SAINTE-MARIE CHAPEL OF THE FILLES
DE LA VISITATION

break across artistic demarcation lines in its search for totality. A calmer, more neo-Classic approach to architecture was preferred.

In 1635 Jacques Lemercier began the church of the Old Sorbonne for Cardinal Richelieu, his chief patron, with the arrangement of buildings round the cour d'honneur, all that is left of his rebuilding of the Sorbonne itself which Richelieu had commissioned in 1629. While recalling a particular Roman Baroque church in plan and dome – Lemercier had studied there (1607–13) and was influenced particularly by Giacomo della Porta – it illustrates well how the French tended to substitute a refined gravity for the more outgoing vigorous qualities of Italian architecture of the period. Yet it is robust as well as elegant and in this is typical of Lemercier.

The plan is ingenious, obtaining an oval effect by setting a circle in a Greek cross at the centre of a longitudinal plan. Unusually, it has two main entrance façades. The one to the front is a two-storey design of superimposed orders (Corinthian and Composite) crowned by a pediment and flanked by volutes over the aisles in the Gesù tradition. It is surmounted at the centre of the church by a fine lanterned dome, raised on a circular drum above pendentives, like a third storey, to see which the Place de la Sorbonne was made in front, an early French example of the Italian Renaissance piazza idea in urban design.

The second entrance façade at the end of the transept overlooking the courtyard is a more original design: a pedimented

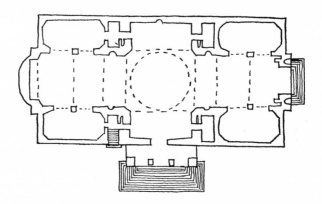

CHURCH OF THE SORBONNE

Corinthian portico – very early – reached up a flight of steps. In the pediment are the Cardinal's arms. Above rises the high-roofed transept with corner turrets and then the tall pilastered drum and ribbed and lantered dome: a splendid conception, both graceful and impressive. Highly successful, too, is the way in which Lemercier achieves effective contrast and balance between the bolder modelling of the lower storey, with strong lights and shadows, and the more delicate linear effects of the upper storey.

This is Lemercier's best building and one of the earliest purely classical of French churches. Mansart and Lemercier are the two architects who were responsible *c.* 1630 for establishing a more correct and purified French Classicism to replace the somewhat over-ornamented Mannerist style which had been most characteristic of the first quarter of the seventeenth century, though Mansart is by far the greater talent – an artist of genius in fact.

CHURCH OF THE SORBONNE

Ten years later than the Sorbonne church F. Mansart began what was originally the church of the Benedictine monastery of the Val-de-Grâce, Paris, another example of French Baroque Classicism, a more sober, more subtle and refined version of the Baroque style than that which had been created in Italy, without its extravagant vigour or complexity, and owing more to Palladio's Il Redentore in Venice.

Later modified when taken over by Lemercier in 1646, it bears some resemblance to the latter's Sorbonne chapel, in that it has a domed exterior with a pedimented façade (1660) of superimposed orders and volutes. There are two storeys and an attic to raise up the pilastered drum, the vertical accents of which have been increased by doubling the number of pilasters and adding statues and candelabra ornament above. Finally the great dome and lantern complete the finely calculated climax, making it one of the most dramatic in all Paris.

The composition is also richer and more elaborate in the way the portico stands forward, almost detached, from the subtly

THE VAL-DE-GRÂCE

balanced façade and in the more vigorous relief. The dome (its enrichment, by the way, was the work of Le Muet, the designer of Notre-Dame-des-Victoires, 1656) was undoubtedly in Wren's mind when he came to design St Paul's.

The interior has a wide nave with flanking piers faced with Corinthian pilasters, a vaulted roof and saucer domes besides the great central dome. There is a magnificent Baroque *baldacchino* with Solomanic columns over the convent chapel altar, and frescoes are features of the wall surfaces. The church is now part of the military hospital; but originally of course it was the heart of the greatest of seventeenth-century French monasteries. The chapel of Saint-Louis, the nun's choir, links it to the complex of conventual buildings – an unmedieval device – consisting essentially of four-storey blocks with classically arcaded groin-vaulted cloisters, pilasters, and pedimented dormers, arranged round a quadrangular court with pavilions at the corners, one for Queen Anne of Austria, with whom the monastery is associated. The exterior of the refectory, however, is still medieval with pointed windows. Thus it may be seen that monastic buildings of this time are generally classical in spirit, like secular architecture, though less elaborate; and there was a tendency towards high building on restricted town sites despite the persistence of court-yard plans.

Other examples of the period are the monasteries of the Port Royal (A. Le Pautre), and of the canons of Sainte-Geneviève, Paris, now the Lycée Henri iv; Saint-Ouen, Rouen; and Saint-Georges, Rennes (1670), with its powerfully designed façade. The façade of the church of the Feuillantes or Reformed Christians, Paris, was one of Mansart's earlier works with Mannerist elements. A far finer work is the chapel of Fresnes, a miniature version of the Val-de-Grâce in some respects and of about the same date.

The preference for a two-tier façade in later centralized churches was probably affected by the desire to make the most of the dome as a strong feature of the external composition. This can be seen again in the chapel of Cardinal Mazarin's Collège des Quatre Nations (1662) – now the Institute de France – by Louis Le Vau, who began as a builder of town houses for rich bourgeoisie and took over at the Louvre after Lemercier's death. Another great essay in French Baroque Classicism, it is his answer to the church of the Sorbonne.

The plan is a Greek cross at the centre of which is an ellipse.

There is an entrance portico and a great dome over the crossing. Spatial imagination is shown in the way the separate elements of the plan are varied. The fact that the site of the College was long and narrow was a handicap but there are two courts. On one side of the cour d'honneur is the chapel, just described, on the other the Bibliothèque Mazarin. The domed chapel forms the centre of the main façade (much of it false) concave to the bank of the River Seine, from which on either hand it is connected to side pavilions by curved wings going back, via Roman Baroque perhaps, to the garden front of Vignola's Villa Giuliana. These pavilions have the new slender type of giant Corinthian pilaster which became characteristic of French classic architecture. Altogether this is a bold and dramatic ensemble best appreciated if approached by the bridge across the river. This dates only from the last century, though a bridge was intended by Le Vau from the beginning.

To accommodate the large numbers of soldiers wounded and disabled as a result of Louis xiv's persistent policies of expansion and conquest, the great military hospital, the Hôtel des Invalides, was built in Paris. In his Second Church of the Invalides F. Mansart's grand-nephew and pupil Jules Hardouin-Mansart continued even more grandly the tradition established by the churches of the Sorbonne and Collège des Quatre Nations.

Saint-Louis (1680) has a centralized plan – an inscribed Greek cross in a square – that is more regularized and spatially less dynamic than the earlier churches. There are four chapels with 'sculptural' walls set in the corners of the square, reached by steps and narrow entrances through the great piers of the powerfully dominating centre space, and an oval chancel which is set

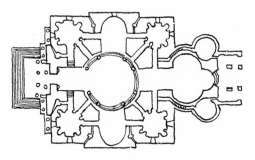

SAINT-LOUIS-DES-INVALIDES

11. Hôtel de Ville, La Rochelle (1595): the Mannerist courtyard of one of the most characteristic secular buildings of the reign of Henri IV. The squat columns, coupled arches, and somewhat coarse detailing produce a rather ponderous effect.

12a. Palais de Versailles: the centre of the garden front of an overwhelming Baroque complex where the architecture, with its horizontal emphasis, extends into the formalised surrounding park landscape. A telling symbol of an aristocratic culture and an absolute monarch.

12b. Château de Vaux-le-Vicomte (1657): a noble but vigorous work by Le Vau. With its short wings, enfilade, oval salon, and mansard roof this is an early French Baroque château where Le Nôtre master-minded the garden planning that culminated at Versailles.

across in a rather Palladian manner. The high altar is a variation
of Bernini's *baldacchino* in St Peter's, Rome. Internally, the
dome – a technical and aesthetic triumph – with its dramatic
concealed lighting of the paintings of the middle dome (it is
actually a triple dome) viewed through the inner, is distinctly
Baroque. Externally, on its two high drums with coupled columns
and high windows, it is a blend of Baroque and classicism:
classical horizontality is modified by Baroque verticality and
exuberance. Here there is a distinction between the Invalides
and the Sorbonne and Val-de-Grâce. Rising by stages above the
façade and finished with sculptured decoration and a strange but
graceful Baroque lantern terminating in a spirelet, it is one of the
most lordly and impressive domes in France. Based on a system
of triangles it illustrates the classical practice of constructing
architectural forms according to geometry and systems of mathe-
matically related proportions.

The two-storey façade is stepped forward through four planes
in a manner which manipulates the massive forms in the Baroque

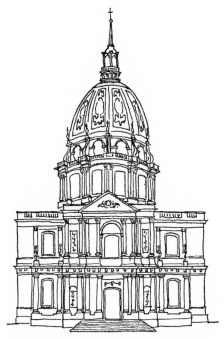

SAINT-LOUIS-DES-INVALIDES

K

spirit, but, characteristically French, it is more rectangular, rational and stoically restrained than its Italian counterparts, except those themselves now showing French influence, as at Turin. The entrance portico has Ionic superimposed on Doric orders and is pedimented. Despite the reserve alluded to and its correctness and sober detail, there is something Baroque in the depth of relief and the way the columns are spaced, and the segment-headed windows are typically French. Altogether this is a splendid and, within its somewhat strict terms of reference, a very individual design that well deserves its high reputation. Under the dome now is the sarcophagus of Napoleon 1 (1842) by Visconti.

These, then, are the five important centralized churches of the seventeenth century in France; but there are of course other lesser examples such as the chapel of the Pénitants Noirs at Villefranche-de-Rouergue (1642) and La Madeleine, Lille (1675) – on a Greek cross plan. Seventeenth-century interiors tended to plainness, Counter-Reformation rather than Baroque in spirit. Thus Daniel Gittard's Saint-Jacques-du-Haut-Pas, Paris, has been called 'the architectural equivalent of Jansenism'. L'Église des Filles de l'Assomption, Paris (1670), is a highly individual version of Baroque of notable severity, however, in its proportionally gigantic drum and dome.

Decorative motifs are classical of course, and sculpture is no longer integral as it was in medieval compositions.

After 1650 there is a return to the basilican plan in classical churches. Lemercier began it with his parish church at Richelieu and at Saint-Roch, Paris (1653) – he also did the Gesù-type Oratoire in Paris – but more typical is Saint-Sulpice (1655) in the same city by Gittard and Le Vau. It is large aisled basilica with radiating chapels; there are eighteen chapels altogether in the church and an external 'chevet' with buttresses. There are thus many medieval echoes despite the classical detailing such as cornices and piers with Corinthian pilasters, which support domical vaulting. The very wide façade like a two-storey narthex has superimposed orders, dates from 1733, and is flanked by late eighteenth-century towers. Also in Paris, Saint-Louis-en-l'Île (1664) by Le Vau, Saint-Nicolas-du-Chardonnet (1656) and Notre-Dame-des-Victoires (1629) belong to the same group. The aisled basilica with radiating plan still appears at the cathedral of Nancy (1706) by J. H. Mansart and Boffrand.

CHÂTEAU DE CHEVERNY

So far we have traced the evolution of the French château from medieval fortress to Early Renaissance country house and royal palace as it had developed by the end of the sixteenth century. Those of the seventeenth and eighteenth century are less well-known, with one or two notable exceptions, but they are equally rewarding to study and very numerous so that only a selection of representative or outstanding examples can be discussed. Cheverny (1634) is an elegant assembly of units each defined by picturesquely varied roof forms while a more compact composition of about 1650 is the Château de Villarceaux, in the Île de France.

Examples of the brick with prominent stone dressings style that came in with Henri IV under Dutch influence are the Normandy châteaux of Balleroy (1626) – by F. Mansart and actually in two sorts of stone – and Beaumesnil (1633), but as we have already seen in the new churches of the seventeenth century a French version of Baroque was being developed for monumental

CHÂTEAU DE VILLARCEAUX

CHÂTEAU DE BALLEROY

buildings from now on. Lemercier's former Château de Rueil and church at Rueil-Malmaison date from about 1630. Lemercier's works in Paris included the new Sorbonne, the Palais-Royal (formerly the Palais-Cardinal, for Richelieu), 1629, and his extensions to the Louvre for Louis XIII.

In 1624 the north and east sides of the old Château du Louvre were demolished and the large Cour Carrée began, very much larger than the medieval court. Lemercier lengthened Lescot's western wing, placed a higher domed Pavillon de l'Horloge at the centre in the earlier style and began the north wing in a more restrained contemporary form of classicism. The Pavillon, independently roofed, is a typical French motif deriving basically from the high medieval tower. Here it was later to inspire the picturesque and dignified additions of the Pavillon Turgot and Pavillon Richelieu.

The north, east, and south sides of the Cour Carrée (including the rebuilding of the Galerie d'Apollon), with arcading on the wall surfaces, were finished for Louis XIV by Le Vau; but the exterior façades were not completed until later. Paris was now becoming the most important architectural centre in Europe – Sir Christopher Wren thought it the best – and Louis XIV invited Bernini, the leading Italian Baroque architect of the day, to design the eastern front of the Louvre, only to set aside his grand conception in favour of a French one.

It is usually ascribed to the versatile Claude Perrault, a typical 'amateur' architect of the period in that he was a physician by profession, as Wren was a scientist; but it may have been the solution more of a committee of which Le Brun, the First Painter and author of the sumptuous decorations of the Galerie d'Apollon (1662), and Le Vau were also members.

Begun in 1667, Perrault's 600 feet long eastern exterior front has a heavy solid podium-like ground storey with tall French segmentally-headed windows, a principal storey with a large free-standing colonnade of rhythmically-spaced slender giant Corinthian columns in pairs, and a balustraded flat Italian roof. There is a pedimented centre-piece and side wings instead of the more usual end pavilions. Colonnade, balustraded flat roof, and the only slightly projecting centre and wings may all owe something to Bernini; though the coupled columns on the podium are ultimately from Bramante and the High Renaissance, their articulation is Roman. Its scale and depth of relief are Baroque but clearly a Baroque without curves.

This palace-front arrangement is a new and significant French departure and there are enough French qualities – for example, the unpedantic elegance despite the nobility, and motifs like the sculptured oval shields and hanging garlands already noted in the ornament on Lescot's work – to endorse the new classic style that is distinctly French with the rationalism of Descartes and the cool grandeur of Poussin.

Despite some criticism of the way the decoration has been applied and of the discords of its prominent chimneys, this is one of the finest classical façades in the world and it was destined to be a very influential work until the end of the eighteenth century.

The best of the exterior façades, it is a most impressive design, impersonally classic and more soberly monumental than the court façades. As Perrault's front was higher than the other façades, so the east side and eastern half of the north and south sides of the court had their attic storeys replaced by a third storey, in contrast

LOUVRE, EAST FRONT

to Lescot's design. The remaining three façades are later, as explained, with a giant order of pilasters instead of a colonnade.

The axis of the courtyard on the west became, as we shall see, the great avenue of the Champs-Élysées reaching out to the country beyond. The south front overlooks the River Seine.

Perrault's writings include a dissertation on the *Ordonnances des Cinq Espèces de Colonne* (1676) and an important translation of Vitruvius with his own scholarly commentary (1684). Another very important treatise was the *Cours d'Architecture* of François Blondel, published from 1675 to 1698, based on his lectures and expounding classical and rationalist principles subscribed to by the Academy.

In the Château de Balleroy (1626), already referred to, François Mansart showed how much he owed to the classicism of de Brosse, combining it with a brick and stone manner of Henri IV's time. Yet, in this typically well-massed, symmetrical and monumental composition with high centre and pavilioned wings, he may also be seen to be moving away from the influence of de Brosse and of Du Cerceau towards his own very personal style. The design is distinguished particularly, too, by the way the entrance is approached by rising levels and curving flights of stairs. Mansart also built the Château de Berny (1624), of which a small part remains, and probably provided the plan for Brécy, executed by a local builder. These too are in Normandy.

His Orléans wing (1635) at the Château of Blois – the centre block and colonnade were to have been part of a larger design not carried through to completion – was commissioned by the King's brother. It well displays the importance of Mansart's contribution to the founding of a French classic style and his great genius for effectively defining and relating masses and achieving proportions of great sensitivity, while exercising remarkable economy of means. It is significant that he made it a cour d'honneur arrangement.

The courtyard entrance is cool and restrained with a two-storey triumphal arch motif. Its three tiers of orders and regular fenestration are well-proportioned and related to the high roof with its tall chimneys. On the third storey the cornice breaks into an original, completely semi-circular pediment – not just a segmental one. At ground floor level elegant curved colonnades screen the angle between the centre block and the short side wings, which go back to de Brosse's Blérancourt.

BLOIS, ORLÉANS WING

The clear-cut detailing of this sophisticated building is characteristically refined and Mansart introduces here the roof of broken pitch – the lower steep, the higher, flatter – which is named after him though he did not invent the type.

The entrance leads through to the splendidly contrived stairwell, dramatically lit and covered by a dome. Open through three floors, it is partly enclosed at the first floor level to accommodate a passage through the building. Noticeable is the general contrast between the earlier work at Blois and the horizontal lines, punctuated by vertical orders and windows, of the rational and polished classicism of Mansart's design.

The most complete of all his works is the great house he built not far from Paris for a *nouveau riche* financier, de Longeuil, who allowed him to revise his design as it progressed, despite the increased costs. This was typical of Mansart and many clients resented it; his genius, however, justified what might have been called vacillation and incompetence in a run-of-the-mill architect. The king and great nobles made little use of him, however; all his clients were of the bourgeoisie whose rapid advancement under Richelieu and Mazarin coincided with the rise of French classicism.

Begun in 1642, three years before he began work on the noble Val-de-Grâce, the Château de Maisons-Laffitte develops the spatial qualities and bold massing already observed at Blois, but the exterior is more boldly modelled. It consists of a long freestanding block with frontispiece – a sophisticated composition of various elements – and flanking wings of equal height. It is therefore an open **E**-shaped plan with no courtyard, which does

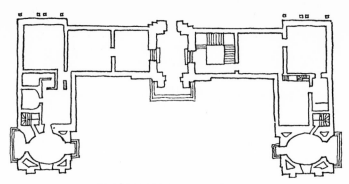

CHÂTEAU DE MAISONS

not follow the Anet tradition, with a fine use of classical orders on the exterior, which is finished off with high roofs and chimney stacks to the three pavilions emphasizing the centre and the two wings. The regular fenestration pattern is unrelated to the interior, as was often the case in classical architecture, where an outward symmetry was so much desired whatever the internal dispositions of the building.

The square stairwell with fine balustraded stairs, covered like Blois with a dome, also has a narrow oval gallery at the first floor level to connect one side of the main block with the other. The effect, however, is less Baroque and more classical. The interior with oval rooms in the vestibule and wings, a shape deriving from Italian Mannerism, is of very special interest since it is the only one of Mansart's to remain unchanged: well-defined spaces with walls, columns, vaults, and sharp restrained ornamental detail, e.g. the chimney pieces, all executed in sober white limestone and unembellished with the more usual gilt-edged panels and paintings. There are, too, notable ornamental ceilings. Here are richness and severity effectively combined, as at the Val-de-Grâce. The final effect of the Château de Maisons is one of civilized reserved grandeur, unpedantic suavity and elegance, clarity and refinement that is distinctively French; at the same time it avoids the French weakness of a formality that tends to dullness. Compared with the Orléans wing it shows the change that affected Mansart's style about this time, when it became freer and more plastic with the earlier rather Mannerist detail giving way to more classical decoration.

In these two monumental works, Blois and Maisons, Mansart,

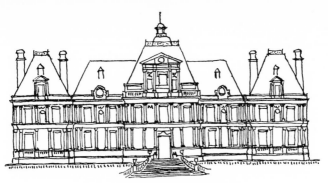

CHÂTEAU DE MAISONS

the most outstanding French architect since Gothic times, and one who as far as we know had never visited Italy, achieves the culmination of the French Renaissance tradition up to that time, unmistakably Classical yet equally unmistakably French. From a foundation to which the work of the Italians Primatticio and Serlio had contributed he evolved a national Baroque classicism that laid more stress on intellectual and visual satisfaction than on the movement and drama of Italian Baroque and became in the process perhaps the greatest of French Renaissance architects and a profound source of influence on the future. He is the Poussin of architecture.

By now the Academies had arrived to confirm and codify classical standards. The French Academy for the visual arts was founded in 1648 and made more powerful in 1663 by Colbert, the chief minister of Louis XIV, who pursued a policy of organizing artistic production and influencing it through institutions so that the arts would serve the French economy and make it more independent of imports, besides raising the country's prestige abroad. Three years later, when Mansart died, the Académie de France in Rome was established (1666). Mansart never went to Rome, as we have said, but now the best students were to be encouraged to absorb the finest lessons of antiquity at its chief Italian source as well as studying the great Renaissance treatises of Alberti, Serlio, Vignola, and Palladio. The academic movement governed intellectual development and laid down standards of taste so that Classicism in France was now to be systematically disciplined. Though not officially founded until 1670 (by Colbert), the Académie d'Architecture became a school of architects drilled in the tradition of French Classic architecture. It is no accident that the age of academies coincides with the growth of a strong centralized absolutist France equally absolutist in matters of art, an attitude at once beneficial and dangerous. Control of French architectural education dates from this time, for the Académie was in due course succeeded by the École des Beaux-Arts.

The second architect after Mansart to share the distinction of laying the foundation of the mature French Classic style was Louis Le Vau. In his great country house of Vaux-le-Vicomte (1657), not far from Paris and built for Fouquet, Louis xiv's Superintendent of Finances, the influence of Italian Baroque (Le Vau had studied in Rome and Genoa), is apparent in the plan, which broadly recalls that of the Palazzo Barberini, Rome, but with shorter wings or corner pavilions behind the cour d'honneur. It is however an early example of what was to become a character-istically French planning arrangement and was adapted from the Château du Raincy which he had designed over ten years before, and which no longer exists. The pale stone elevations express the plan admirably, but the orders are very loosely used.

The interior, axially orientated, is designed with rooms care-fully related to one another. This is the first 'enfilade' or suite of rooms in line, to produce a vista through their connecting doors. At the centre of the main block, two rooms deep and stepped out from a three-arched entrance towards the wings, is a very fine reception suite consisting of an oblong vestibule and large oval grand salon covered with a sturdy dome, about which are grouped the high angular French roofs of the pavilions or wings. The splendid salon overlooking the garden, for which Le

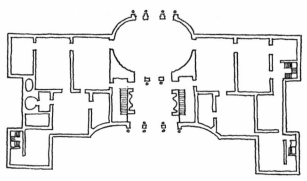

VAUX-LE-VICOMTE

Brun did the paintings and the stocco decoration, was much copied in the Germanic countries during the next century. The pavilions have a new slender type of colossal Corinthian pilaster already noticed – like the oval motif of the salon – at Le Vau's church of the Collège des Quatre Nations, but actually later in date than these here at Vaux-le-Vicomte. They run up through two storeys. The motif is not new in France by this time, but the elegant slimness is; it may owe something to the manner of the Maurithuis, The Hague (1633) by Jakob van Kampen. Despite the small-scale domesticity of the latter, it had behind it the prestige of Holland at the height of its powers. The Château of Vaux-le-Vicomte was Le Vau's best opportunity and he made the most of it with a fine forceful design. Other examples of his châteaux are Seignelay and Bercy, a late work of 1670, besides his extensions to Vincennes.

In the park surrounding the Château of Vaux-le-Vicomte André Le Nôtre first put his ideas for garden design into full effect. A landscape architect as much as a garden designer, Le Nôtre sought for grand unified effects. Thus the main axes of the layout are related to the house; there are terraces at different levels, green spaces of grass, broad parterres of flowers defined by hedges contrasted with masses of trees, radiating avenues, and pools and fountains to provide focal points. All these principles he was to exercise again later at Versailles – that climax of *le grand siècle* – where he realized them even more thoroughly and on a more magnificent scale.

Fit for a king – who soon disposed of its owner – Vaux-le-Vicomte is the most significant and grandest of the non-royal châteaux. It saw the first large-scale collaboration of Le Vau, the painter Le Brun, the sculptor Guerin, and Le Nôtre. It was this combination that was to be responsible for the great developments soon to follow at Versailles and to which we now turn.

Versailles was not only a royal palace or court residence – though it was intended to be, and was, the most imposing achievement of this kind in the world, with accommodation for thousands. It was also a symbol of the highly organized and centralized power of the Sun-King and the vast headquarters of government, the huge rational administration which had been built up in France by the second half of the seventeenth century at a time when she had assumed the role of arbiter of European taste and manners. Its achievement is not in novelty and innovation but in the co-ordination of existing ideas on an unprecedented scale, an essentially Baroque unity of all the arts directed towards a single purpose in the grand manner.

Versailles began in 1624 as a small hunting lodge built perhaps by de Brosse for Louis XIII, Louis XIV's father – a brick building with stone dressings and high roof of the type seen in the Place des Vosges, arranged quadrangularly round the Cour de Marbre facing the town.

In 1669, Le Vau, now the leading architect of the time, and one unusually responsive to Italian ideas for a Frenchman, began to remodel and enlarge this earlier building by adding two flat-roofed wings ending in porticoes as lateral extensions of the Cour de Marbre; and on the garden side he built a great Baroque central block with massive arcaded ground floor, above which level the centre of the façade was recessed, and provided a raised terrace and fountain.

The Collège Mazarin, Vaux-le-Vicomte and his work at Versailles show clearly that Le Vau was the leading Baroque architect in France, with a gift for splendid planning and decorative effects and an ability to create a *mise-en-scène*; on the other hand his typical fault is in detailing.

Le Vau also laid out in an 'absolutist' scheme the streets east of the Palace of Versailles itself. The latter has a history that

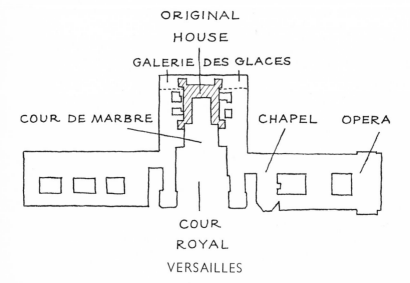

ORIGINAL

HOUSE

GALERIE DES GLACES

COUR DE MARBRE   CHAPEL   OPERA

COUR

ROYAL

VERSAILLES

involves several phases of development, and in contrast to Le Vau's work, which sometimes appears rather heavy with ungainly proportions, that of Jules Hardouin-Mansart, who trebled its size, from 1678 is on an even vaster scale and marks a change to a calmer, less plastic, more rational and static neo-Classical manner with a distinct emphasis on the horizontal. The enormous size of the palace and its vast spread, however, remain as essentially Baroque characteristics. Mansart, who dominated the second half of Louis XIV's reign, was a very able architect, clever and adaptable, if not as exacting in his aesthetic standards as the greatest. He had a real gift for anticipating the needs of the King's ceremonial and a natural dramatic sense, qualities which helped him quickly to become his favourite architect and to gain him, eventually, the directorship of the Academies of Painting, Sculpture, and Architecture and a patent of nobility.

His early work, e.g. the Château du Val and the Château de Clagny (1674) for the King's mistress, Mme de Montespan, show a debt to Le Vau rather than his grand-uncle but also an untypical proto-Rococo ingenuity and variety in planning and a new horizontal emphasis.

Thus, though they owe something to Le Vau's monumental forms and motifs, the present immense north (1684) and south façades (1679) of the garden front, set back a little and stretching out for over a quarter of a mile, are by Hardouin-Mansart who replaced the terrace over the ground floor of the centre by a horizontal gallery linking the wings, thus filling in the middle of the design. Despite the free-standing portico at the first floor level, however, the composition lacks a centre piece capable of focusing and dominating such an extensive spread of front. This lack of a unifying feature necessary to a classically conceived work of architecture is a criticism which has frequently been levelled at Versailles and the defect is one which may be traced right back to the early history of the palace.

The repetitiveness, too, of these façades, lacking strong articulation and with an order scaled to a shorter design, and the unbroken skyline, which leads to monotony, detract from the impressiveness of the extravagant scale of the design; but it is only fair to say that closer to, the façades are much more successful compositions. Then details of the well-proportioned rusticated ground floor, supporting an order of Ionic columns, the tall round-headed windows of the main storey, the high attic and

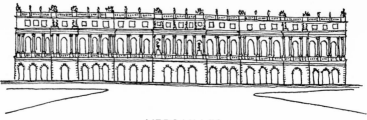

VERSAILLES

balustrade may be properly used and enjoyed. This is in contrast to the general rule at Versailles, where – with the important exception noted – the overall impression so often succeeds in overcoming particular weaknesses. The change of style from Le Vau to J. H. Mansart is also noticeable in the latter's modification to the Cour de Marbre.

In their decorative scheme for the *Grands Appartements* of the King and Queen – the iconographical theme was appropriately enough Apollo or the Sun – Le Vau and Le Brun abandoned the panelling of Louis XIII's reign, preferring instead a richer Italian style. Though still 'architecturally' employed, it consisted of stucco ceilings with paintings, walls hung with patterned velvet or covered with polychrome marbles, and marble floors, now vanished, and furnishings of inlay, gilt bronze and silver.

Le Brun, a painter and not an architect, was head of the royal factory at Paris at the Hôtel des Gobelins, which now embraced the whole range of interior furnishing and acted as a training school. He occupied the position of artistic director or co-ordinator, and when J. H. Mansart succeeded Le Vau the same type of rich decoration was continued in the new interiors, though even more effectively, as may be seen especially in the new and extravagant Galerie des Glaces (1678) – linking the Salons de la Guerre and de la Paix – with its large mirrors (an advertisement for French industry) and windows separated by Corinthian pilasters of green marble with capitals of Le Brun's French order bearing an entablature surmounted by trophies. The ceiling is decorated with painted panels showing the apotheosis of *le Roi Soleil*.

Coysevox, the sculptor, also worked in both the Galerie des Glaces and in the Salon de la Guerre. The silver furniture which must have been an important element in the rich effect, like that of the *Grand Appartement*, was soon melted down to pay for Louis' military extravagance.

This time it is the interior which shows the Baroque Classicism associated with his reign. These grand rooms – Baroque in disposition, more classical in detail – together with the Salle des Gardes de la Reine, the Salon de l'Œil-de-Bœuf (1701) and the Escalier de la Reine offer fine examples of craftsmanship and interior design, but the best part of Le Brun's earlier decoration, for the Escalier des Ambassadeurs by Le Vau (a Spanish T-plan type staircase introduced to France for the first time here), with its Baroque opulence and illusionism no longer exists as it was destroyed by Louis xv, along with other parts, to create *petits appartements* more suited to the style of life of a later generation.

Even in Louis xiv's reign, after 1684 smaller rooms show a change in the style of interior decoration, for the ornate coloured marbles and gilt bronze are set aside in favour of painted and gilt-edged panelling more usually associated with the early eighteenth century.

If Hardouin-Mansart tended to defer to Le Vau's example somewhat when he followed him in the garden façades, in one of his most successful works, the Royal Chapel (1699) he allowed himself to be more individual and his style changed again towards a less disciplined, more elegantly exuberant manner. The chapel is longitudinal in plan, with an apse the full height and width of the unified interior, which has a gallery with Corinthian columns supported on piers. The gallery dominates over the arcade ground storey as this was where the King sat and it leads directly to the royal *appartement*; the ceiling is decorated with a splendid Baroque illusionist painting by Coypel. The chapel's tall proportions, like its roof and external flying buttresses, show a link between Gothic and Rococo, but the way the light from the triple tier of tall windows bathes the interior is more characteristic of the latter. In Rococo the robustness of earlier interior spaces is transformed into something more restrained and elegant. But we are anticipating the developments of the next century described in the next chapter. J. H. Mansart's brother-in-law Robert de Cotte completed the chapel and the detailing is superb. Besides influencing the German Rococo, de Cotte did the Hôtel de Bouvallais, Paris (1717) and about the same time was responsible for the brilliant Rococo gallery in F. Mansart's Hôtel de la Vrillière. At Strasbourg he built the episcopal palace.

Reference has already been made to Le Nôtre's principles of garden design in connection with Vaux-le-Vicomte. In accordance with them, and on an even vaster scale, he laid out the garden park at Versailles (1667) as an integral part of the total scheme, extending the symmetry of the palace into the surrounding landscape. Baroque planning contrives three wide approach roads from the town side to focus on the cour d'honneur of the entrance front, *via* the Place d'Armes and the Cour Royale, while on the other side a great vista, leading the eye two miles to the horizon, and a grand canal continue the main axis of the palace through the vast garden and park. Balanced masses of trees are cut through by avenues and offer clear-cut contrasts of light and shade with the parterres near the palace and, further away, green spaces of lawns. There is an assured combination of natural and artificial elements: groves of trees, the Tapis-Vert, the still surfaces of ornamental pools, punctuated by fountains, classical statues, and antique vases, all skilfully composed to make a superb setting for the outdoor amusements and fêtes of the Court. Colour effects were not considered important or particularly desirable, odd as that might seem to the modern gardener. One recalls that this was the time of the drawing *versus* colour controversy in painting, when the orthodox academicians supported drawing as the more intellectual, though rationalism was the dominant theme of the period, from the economic theory of Colbert to Bossuet's theology. Le Nôtre's is an impressive formal, some might say rigid, scheme carefully and precisely planned and cultivated. It perfectly expresses that control over nature which seventeenth-century garden design sought to achieve, subduing all the elements of architecture and garden into one ordered and integrated symmetrical plan. As son of the gardener of the Tuileries and a student of architecture and painting, Le Nôtre had the ideal training to bring this about. The similarity between the formality of this sort of arrangement and the strict formality of the Court is not likely to be overlooked. As an essay in Baroque planning its influence was felt far afield, not only in the design of parks *à la française*, but also subsequently in town planning as the layout of Washington, D.C. makes clear.

Le Nôtre, a member of the French academy, also laid out gardens at Marly, Chantilly and Saint-Cloud, besides remodelling those at Fontainebleau and the Tuileries. He was responsible, too, for initiating the grand prospect of the famous Avenue des Champs-Élysées leading from the gardens of the Tuileries to the horizon.

GRANDES ÉCURIES, CHANTILLY

Le Vau did the Orangery at Versailles, J. H. Mansart the New Orangery and stables. The latter also built the Grand Trianon or Trianon de Marbre (1687) which replaced Le Vau's little pavilion Trianon in the park, where the royal family could escape from the pomp, publicity, and overwhelming vastness of Versailles and relax from court etiquette. Again Hardouin-Mansart worked with de Cotte producing a one-storey villa, on the pattern of the main palace, with a central ground floor loggia. Despite its rather purer classic grandeur, the planning, asymmetrical and freer, and the decoration show a shift towards Rococo. The cathedral of Versailles is by a grandson of Hardouin-Mansart.

Altogether the palace of Versailles is an extravagant and ostentatious expression of the monarchy which had made seventeenth-century France the richest, most powerful, and in many ways the most prestigious country in the world. Royal building projects at this time were the responsibility of what was in fact an entire special ministry with a labour force running into tens of thousands of building workers and craftsmen of all sorts. Notwithstanding its monumental grandeur, perhaps Versailles' greatest qualities are the high level of integration it achieves between architecture, garden and interior design; and the abundance of splendid craftsmanship which it displays. It is not surprising that France led Europe during this period in the quality of its furniture, tapestries and textiles.

A number of other notable châteaux were built about this time not far from Versailles, among them Saint-Cloud – only the beautiful gardens survive – and Marly (now destroyed), the latter, by J. H. Mansart, a charmingly laid-out group of small pavilions for King and courtiers in a Versailles-like park. The same architect's Dampierre (1675) with its central corps de logis and flanking, detached, side blocks shows the characteristic French Baroque arrangement round a cour d'honneur, copied all over Europe. But in general one architecturally significant result of the building of Versailles and the establishment of the system of centralized absolutism which it represented was that the nobility of France gravitated to it, and there were fewer country houses built from the 1660's until after the Revolution. No doubt the great cost of Louis XIV's unsuccessful later campaigns also contributed to the lack of funds available for building purposes.

Towards the end of the Wars of Religion and the beginning of the seventeenth century the classic type of *hôtel particulier* or large detached town house for noblemen or rich bourgeois began to emerge. They were especially characteristic of Paris and each period had its fashionable quarter.

Basically seventeenth-century plans consist of a main block flanked by two side service wings, i.e. the half-**H**-plan enclosing a quadrangular forecourt, called the cour d'honneur when a base court for services and stabling was added at the side. The fourth side of the forecourt was screened from the street by a wall with an entrance gateway. On the far side of the corps de logis, which overlooked it, extended the garden. This was the type known as the 'hôtel entre cour et jardin', positioned like Mazarin's Opera at the Tuileries.

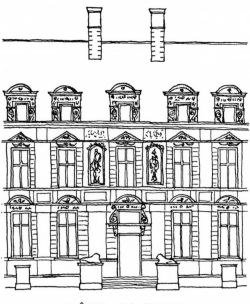

HÔTEL DE SULLY

Early seventeenth-century examples in Paris include the Hôtel de Mayenne (1605) by Jacques Androuet Du Cerceau the Younger; the symmetrical and richly decorated Hôtel de Sully (1624) by Jean Du Cerceau, grandson of the Elder; the Hôtel de Liancourt (1623) by Lemercier, an ingeniously planned house of extensive influence; and the entirely classical hôtel built by F. Mansart in 1635 which became the Banque de France in 1812. It is another subtle and very influential design in which the emphasis is on symmetry and simplicity.

The Hôtel de Liancourt illustrates the way, in subsequent designs, corner and diagonal entrances from the cour d'honneur were sometimes used to avoid difficulties caused by the fact that different parts of the building were planned on different axes.

The trend towards a greater variety and number of rooms and the introduction of curved shapes may be studied in the plan of the Hôtel Lambert (1639) by Le Vau, much finer than the earlier examples, with its oval vestibule, octagonal rooms, rounded angles, and magnificent Hercules Gallery (1648) with frescoes by Le Brun and stucco work by Van Obstal. Superbly decorated and taking advantage of the views, especially from its terminal bow window, this is one of the very finest of a type of gallery not uncommon in Parisian houses. The grandiloquent staircase is

HÔTEL LAMBERT

theatrically conceived and very original and the whole plan cleverly related to the excellent site on the Île Saint-Louis.

The main entrance from the cour d'honneur is through a triple-arched portico carried up through both storeys – a characteristic Le Vau motif, cf. Vaux-le-Vicomte – and the corners are made concave. The inconsistent use of orders externally shows that Le Vau thought in terms of decorative façades rather than in masses like F. Mansart.

The highly inventive Hôtel de Beauvais, Paris (1652) by Antoine Le Pautre has even more curved lines and plan shapes in its masterly handling of a very irregular double site to obtain effects both of symmetry and of novel disposition. Towards the end of the century these gave way to more angular designs in the grander and more elaborate houses, e.g. Pierre Cottard's Hôtel des Ambassadeurs de Hollande (1657) with its specially fine porte-cochère. The magnificent Hôtel Aubert de Fontenay (1656) is an isolated work by the hand of Jean Boullier.

Under the retarded influence of Du Cerceau the Elder, Pierre Le Muet (who published designs for some quite small private houses) did the somewhat Mannerist Hôtel Duret de Chevry, Paris (1635), now absorbed into the Bibliothèque Nationale,

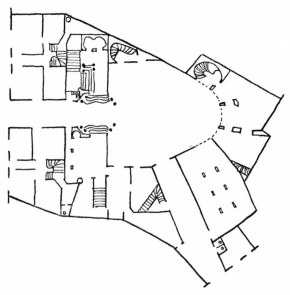

HÔTEL DE BEAUVAIS

while the Hôtel de Beaumont, Valognes, has a curving Baroque façade that is yet typically French in its sobriety and restraint. Turning now from the domestic architecture of the seventeenth century to other secular buildings of the period, one finds a number of notable hôtels de ville including Marseille, Toulon (1656), Arles, and the belfried example at Lyon (rebuilt by Hardouin-Mansart in 1674), wîth its impressive entrance and cour d'honneur, which stands in the Place des Terreaux together with the Palais de Saint-Pierre (1667) by La Vafrenière.

Jacques Bruant's classical façade of the Drapers' Hall (c. 1655) may be seen in the Musée Carnavalet. It is one of the few public buildings of its time and is basically like the style of F. Mansart, though also intended as a sculptural display.

Hospitals follow the medieval precedent of building round courtyards but do so in more elaborate and varied ways, adopting the style of the time for façades and detail. Claude Chastillon's Hôpital Saint-Louis, Paris (1607) was an isolation hospital attached to the Hôtel-Dieu. The planning is ingenious, since the arrangement is one of several spaced enclosures with patients round the centre court cut off from the outside by staff quarters, washhouses, and kitchen blocks. In the chapel, nave and choir are segregated; and in the hospital itself the use of revolving hatches permits communication with the inner parts.

But the greatest seventeenth-century hospital is of course the Invalides, begun in 1671 before J. H. Mansart's church, known by that name, which stands behind it. Here Libéral Bruant, Jacques's

HÔTEL DE VILLE, LYON: ENTRANCE

brother, has placed the courts side by side. The long main façade is classical but without orders, a solemn four-storey composition, restrained to the point of severity, and thus anticipating the spirit of neo-classicism, with high roof and dormer windows decorated with battle trophies. The centre pavilion stands higher and is dominated by a huge curved pediment motif.

The cour d'honneur in the centre has a two-storey colonnade framing the Soldiers' Church. This has Roman gravity but again there is the high roof and dormers and in the middle of each side a slight triangular pedimented projection marking the axis. Large and self-contained, it was an effective architectural solution within the terms of its time. That these were often too restricting is clear from Perrault's design for the astronomer Cassini's Observatoire, Paris (1667), where the needs of the new science were neglected for the demands of the classical canon.

The Hôtel des Invalides accommodated seven thousand patients; the other great Hôpital de la Salpêtrière (1656) nearly four thousand. For this also Bruant had designed a centrally planned domed church, to which the wards were connected. It was very originally planned in a manner which excelled J. H. Mansart's work in this respect and has the air of simplicity characteristic of Bruant.

The apartment house has a long history in France and early examples may be seen in the rue François Miron, near Saint-Gervais. So has engineering architecture, and in this field the greatest master of fortification was Louis XIV's faithful Sebastienne de Vauban, whose work still survives in part in what were some of the greatest fortresses in Europe that saved France from invasion after the defeat of her armies in the field. Vauban made fortification a science and at Neuf-Brisach in Alsace, guarding the Rhine, were defences in great depth, ideally developed on a level site. The plan is a centralized geometrical one with bastioned towers (introduced by Vauban), pointed bastions and demi-lunes, surrounded by moats and glacis slopes, all the parts being swept by cross fire and commanded from within. Neuf-Brisach (1698) is perhaps Vauban's finest achievement in fortification but it also shows his approach to planning and his architectural style. Longwy was originally another of his planned towns, and in the south-east are the ramparts of Briançon.

This brings us again to the subject of urban design. The first *places royales* instigated by Henri IV in the earliest years of the

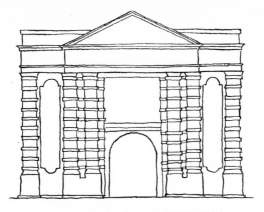

NEUF-BRISACH, GATEWAY

seventeenth century have already been described in the previous chapter. In this it remains to note the new town of Richelieu in Touraine (1631) consistently planned on rational principles by Lemercier for the powerful cardinal of that name – with its great château (of which only fragments remain) church, grid-plan, and uniform housing of brick-with-stone dressings style favoured in the thirties – and to consider the development of town planning which took place in the later seventeenth century in the reign of Louis XIV. These developments were based on the concept of the centralized 'square' but leading to a greater variety of shapes than this term suggests. Four-storeyed façades, as before, conformed to the general scheme; but now the two storeys above the basement were made markedly unequal in height, and a royal statue provided a point of focus.

Jules Hardouin-Mansart, whose other principal architectural works have been dealt with, was responsible for the circular Place des Victoires (1675), once deliberately isolated from the traffic circulation of the city and ennobled with magnificent palace-front façades decked out with classical orders. In the brash stridency of the twentieth century it is difficult to realize what must have been its original calm and aloofness.

The width of Hardouin-Mansart's dignified yet spectacular squares was related to the height of the façades facing them as it was appreciated that these could best be viewed at an angle of 18 degrees – another example of the mathematical relationships behind classical architecture and urban design.

J. H. Mansart's Place Vendôme (1698) is a rectangle with chamfered corners, and though its architectural qualities are better preserved, the present column – replacing Girardon's equestrian statue of the king – is out of proportion and the great vistas of its only two exits have gone. Exits were deliberately restricted in number or masked, to isolate such squares and to afford opportunities for vista effects so much admired in classical Renaissance planning. Usually these were terminated by a prominent building, monument, or other strong accent.

Essentially this was conceived as a restrained Baroque *mis-en-scène* to the glory of the king, for it was to be surrounded by royal establishments and in this lay a marked contrast to the more socially useful intention of Henri IV in his royal squares; Mansart's intention was more single-minded.

One of the planning schemes of Henry IV had been that for the Place de France, from which long, straight, radiating streets had been projected in the manner of those constructed in Sistine Rome in the late sixteenth century. It was this that became the native germ of the central Baroque planning of Louis XIV's reign with its ronds-points as exemplified by the Place des Victoires and the Place Vendôme, and above all by the lay-out of Versailles by Le Nôtre. Seventeenth-century ideas are expressed in his design for the town as well as for the park: three avenues converge on the palace; three on the grand canal. Symmetry rules.

It was at Versailles about this time that J. H. Mansart did a circular design for the Bosquet de la Colonnade and, to provide an approach for his church of Notre-Dame there, the Place Hoche, a square with chamfered corners.

At Dijon he did the Place Royale, now the Place de la Libération, but of the several provincial developments in the decades about 1700 the best are probably the Place Bellecour, Lyon; the Promenade du Peyrou, Montpellier, with a triumphal arch gateway following the Porte Saint-Denis and the Porte Saint-Martin; and above all the square by Jacques Gabriel at Rennes (1721), which will be our starting point for discussion of eighteenth-century urban design in France, with its themes of the development of related groups of squares, of greater freedom and openness in planning. These then were the chief models for eighteenth-century squares throughout Europe and together with ideas of Baroque planning were the main French contribution to classical urban designs which persisted well into the nineteenth century.

CHAPTER SEVEN

The Eighteenth Century

THE great town houses of the eighteenth century evolved continuously from those of the seventeenth. One of the most ingenious architects of hôtels was Pierre Bullet, a contemporary of J. H. Mansart and the architect of the Port Saint-Denis and the Porte Saint-Martin of the 1670's. Though a pupil of F. Blondel, in his plans for the Hôtel Crozat and the Hôtel d'Evreux at the corner of the Place Vendôme (especially in the latter with its clever diagonal approach to the regular cour d'honneur), he laid the foundations of Rococo planning, as distinct from decoration. In his domestic work away from Versailles Mansart made a similar contribution in varied, more fluent planning.

The eighteenth century rounded off the outer corners of the courtyard, reduced the projection of the wings and doubled the width of the main block. Exteriors, like plans, were variations on the basic theme. Classical orders, first applied to a private town house in the Hôtel Lamoignon, Paris, were characteristic but not essential. Sculptured pediments and keystones and fine wrought iron balconies were also features, and at the end of the century neo-Classical friezes were introduced along the upper parts of the design, as in the Hôtel de Salm, now the Chancellerie de la Légion d'Honneur (1782) by Pierre Rousseau.

As regards interior planning, early examples show solemn enfilades of rooms and no separation between their functions apart from the hall. Thus bedrooms were also reception rooms. But later, as the hall disappeared, specialized rooms came in: dining rooms, drawing rooms, boudoirs and libraries. Various ante-rooms such as dressing rooms, closets, and alcoves also diversified the plan, of which the main elements were the vestibule, main staircase, and gallery or drawing room. There was, too, a tendency to put the main reception rooms on the ground floor with the private rooms upstairs. These changes were associated with the Louis xv period when there were marked advances in the art of civilized living, illustrated by great achievements in the applied arts as well as in the cultural dominance of the Paris *salons* – now that the influence of Versailles had declined – where philosophy, literature, and politics were so fruitfully discussed under the patronage of distinguished women, intellectual as well as fashionable.

In music Couperin and Rameau had succeeded the great Lully. Significantly both were outstanding masters of the clavecin, essentially a chamber instrument – whatever else their musical talents led them to be – and were Frenchmen in a way the Florentine never was.

In the eighteenth-century French hôtel the gallery was displaced as the main reception room by the drawing room, and reception rooms were grouped at the centre of a suppler type of plan with other rooms disposed around. Enfilades being dispensed with, similar effects were now obtained by the use of tall looking glasses. Corridors and staircases mutiplied, e.g. the Hôtel de Bourbon, Paris. The staircase had to be suitably impressive but also functional and unobstructive. The usual type was corbelled out from the wall supported by arches, an elegant open type deriving from Palladio by Mansart that became typically French.

A particular problem of hôtel planning was how to preserve symmetry in the two fronts of the main block when they did not share a single axis and in the Hôtel Matignon, Paris (1726) by Jean Courtonne, with its restrained and unmonumental exterior, it is noticeable how the ingeniously arranged cabinets and smaller rooms and service courts obtain symmetrical effects, while at the same time they provide for the necessary functional needs of the household.

The tendency, then, as these hôtels continued to develop until the end of the eighteenth century, was for their plans to grow ever more complicated, inventively contrived, and delicately

HÔTEL MATIGNON

detailed. Façades continued in some form of classicism though more elegant and less severe; storeys were more articulated and their windows grew in number. There was not the same inclination to reflect changes in fashion, however, as in interior décor and it is usual to find a somewhat strictly classical exterior contrasting with a Rococo interior; outward gravity, inward expressiveness, as in de Cotte's Hôtel d'Estrées.

Seventeenth-century interiors, of which those preserved in Le Vau's Hôtel de Lauzun, Paris (1655) are good examples, were dominated by large columns and paintings, but in the eighteenth century these latter were limited to panels, such as J. H. Fragonard's work at the Hôtel de Matignon already mentioned. In the Hôtel de Beauvais, about 1710–15, was evolved a lighter, more playful type of carved wood and gilded stucco framing of wall panels and mirrors. This was the beginning of the decorative style which became known as Rococo and in which the boldness and grandeur of Baroque was brilliantly developed by a number of superb decorators into a highly organized mode characterized by lively, graceful, fanciful forms in resilient three-dimensional curves.

From about 1720, then, reflecting the gayer, more refined and self-indulgent mood of the Regence and the reign of Louis xv, decoration begins to sport sinuous forms, *rocaille* and arabesques – deriving from *grotteschi* ornament – that are associated with the Rococo style. The term itself was actually first applied to the ornament used at Hardouin-Mansart's Marly by Pierre Le Pautre in the early years of the eighteenth century, and *rocaille* signifies 'rockwork', as in the grottoes of Versailles; possibly the contemporary vogue for *chinoiserie* contributed to its typical motifs.

Undoubtedly the finest example of it in Paris are the interiors of the Hôtel de Soubise (*c.* 1730) by Germain Boffrand, the architect who with de Cotte spanned the period between the reigns of Louis xiv and Louis xv and did most to form the full Rococo style, of which his light, elegant Salon Ovale is a magnificent specimen. The building itself, severely classical but relieved by sculpture, is earlier (1705) and is by Pierre-Alexis Delamair, who designed the fine Hôtel de Rohan; though Boffrand, a pupil of J. H. Mansart, had a very large hôtel practice, e.g. the Hôtel Amelot (1710) round an oval court with restrained exterior and luxurious interior, a post-Baroque arrangement. Almost always, Rococo effects, which naturally clashed with the classical ideals and rules of the Academy, were confined to interior schemes of decoration. But though interior only reluctantly followed façades, under Louis xvi they too become more restrained, straighter lines ousting the curves of Rococo and classical motifs (columns, garlands, and panniers) reappearing. After 1770, under the influence of Charles Louis Clérisseau, the designer and student of Italian antiquities who visited Spalato with our own Robert Adam, a more Romantic Classical style became fashionable with pale colours, less gilt, and a variety of archaic sources for its motifs: Egyptian, Etruscan, and Pompeian art. After the Revolution this style became even more austerely classical and plainer – the Directoire style; though during the Empire period some of the richer ornament returned, a new sumptuousness matching Napoleon's more showy taste.

Well-proportioned dignified apartment houses of the eighteenth century still survive in cities like Bordeaux and Rennes and may be seen in Paris in the rue Saint-Honoré and Place St. Sulpice, where they are rather grand and elaborate compared with the mid-Georgian town house of the same time.

Architectural Rococo is uncommon in France and is mostly found in the work done in the eastern provinces by and under the influence of Germain Boffrand and Emmanuel Héré for Stanislas Leczinski, the King's father-in-law, ex-King of Poland and Duke of Lorraine.

Though he never visited Paris, Héré created at Nancy (1751) one of the finest essays in town planning design in France, a major conception which despite its axial planning is very Rococo

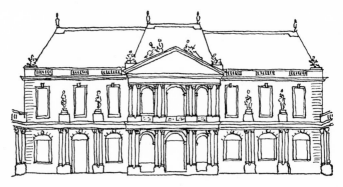

HÔTEL DE SOUBISE

in spirit; it develops its various elements with a new and exciting freedom that is both sophisticated and capriciously original.

Héré's scheme was to link up the old town of Nancy with the new development on the other side of the demolished fortifications – it still has some medieval gateways – and he did this by devising a varied sequence of three squares which run from the Hôtel de Ville to the Palais de l'Intendance. The effect has been likened to a series of immense outdoor staterooms. First came the oval space in front of the new palace in the old town, the Hémicycle with its transverse curving colonnades. This opened to the Place de la Carrière, a long rectangle in plan enclosed by uniform façades and lined down its centre with rows of trees. Next came a triumphal arch gateway leading over a bridge to the Place Louis xv, now the Place Stanislas, a magnificent square with a statue at the centre and entrances at the corners with splendid ornamental wrought iron gates by Jean Lamour, who was out-standing among the fine French craftsmen of the period who worked in that medium producing richly designed gates, railings, balconies and banisters.

Unfortunately the châteaux built for Stanislas have since been demolished or have had their original interiors and gardens removed so that they are only shadows of their former glory.

There are Rococo elements in the Abbey of Prémontré in the Aisne region, and the similarity between the interior of Le Vau's Saint-Louis-en-l'Île, Paris, and the contemporary salon is too obvious to miss.

Jacques Jules Gabriel was a notable builder of hôtels, for example the Hôtel Peyrenc de Moras (Biron), now the Musée Rodin, and the Hôtel Varangeville (1707), and of bridges, for example Blois, Lyon, Poissy, Pontoise, besides the palace of the Archbishop at Blois (1725) and the Hôtel de Ville, Rennes (1734). He was a scholarly architect who capped a successful career by becoming Premier Architecte and Director of the Academy.

The most distinguished architect to emerge in France, and indeed Europe, towards the middle of the eighteenth century was his son Ange-Jacques Gabriel, whose work at Versailles we shall now consider. After the death of Louis xiv the court removed from Versailles under the *Régence* of the Duc d'Orléans, but later Louis xv transferred it again to its former home and proceeded to carry out his own ideas there. We have seen how he had the wonderful Escalier des Ambassadeurs removed.

The wing of the Cour de Marbre containing it was demolished by Gabriel and replaced by his own design in 1742. Later still, wishing to preserve the symmetry of this entrance court, Louis-Philippe in the nineteenth century had the other wing rebuilt on similar lines; its colonnades and pediments recall Perrault's Louvre front, looking back, as Gabriel did, to the period before the advent of Rococo.

The recently restored Opéra (1753) at Versailles is a sumptuously elegant design by Gabriel, whose work concluded this great monument and epitome of the Golden Age of French architecture; but probably better known is his Petit Trianon (1762), a small elegant villa that moves away from earlier part of the century's curves and Rococo tendency to a more severe and disciplined type of neo-classicism more likely to win the approval of the Academy; it is a style, neo-classicism, that becomes pronounced from c. 1760 and though associated chiefly with the reign of Louis XVI it clearly begins before that. Gabriel would have remodelled the whole of Versailles in it had he been allowed to. It shows Gabriel to be essentially conservative, carrying on the classical tradition of F. Mansart. The Petit Trianon may owe something to English Palladianism. It was designed for Mme du Barry, a clean-cut cubical block with rusticated basement and giant order of Corinthian pilasters running through the upper storeys. The façades are related to the dispositions of the interior which show the eighteenth century's turning away from the more pompous formality of Louis XIV's time to a type of planning

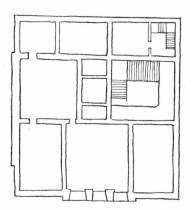

THE PETIT TRIANON, VERSAILLES

THE PETIT TRIANON, VERSAILLES

that is better suited to the functional and domestic needs. The palace, for example, had no dining room but the Petit Trianon had both a salon and a dining room with a table that could be elevated, from the kitchen below, already set.

Outside, the Petit Trianon is cleverly related to the garden with stairs leading from the centre bay of the free-standing Corinthian columns to the curved terrace which embraces it. Dignified and harmonious with exquisite proportions and adjustments, it is the best domestic example of Gabriel's tranquil and sophisticated classicism, which reflects the stability of the French social order of the period, just as the décor of the time mirrors its essential aristocratic frivolity – despite the existence of a small but important intellectual élite.

Eighteenth-century interiors may be seen in Gabriel's apartments for Louis XV and Richard Mique's for Marie-Antoinette. The salon in the Petit Trianon is typical of Louis Quinze – a less severe taste than that prevailing when most of the palace had been built – with panelled walls, gilt-edged, double doors, consoled chimney piece, mirrored walls, and coved ceiling. Chandalier and furniture are also of the period, which it should be remembered

PALACE OF COMPIÈGNE

was one in which the cabinet maker's art was at its most fertile and creative in the number and variety of designs it produced *Rocaille* ornament, sinuous and fretted, was characteristic here also. As well as at Versailles, most of Gabriel's time was spent on making other neo-classic additions and alterations to the palaces of Marly, Compiègne (1752) and Fontainebleau, e.g. the pavilion for Mme de Pompadour at Fontainebleau, known as the Hermitage (1748) – a perfect small gem of a building. The Petit Château at Choisy-le-Roi (1754) shows him leading up to his peak of achievements in the Petit Trianon at Versailles, where he also did the Pavillon Français (1750).

Before taking final leave of Versailles, the best of which was such a great source of inspiration for neo-classic architecture of the early twentieth century, e.g. Reginald Blomfield's Regent Street which, unhappily, replaced Nash's original, let us look briefly at the rest of the work Mique did there for the ill-fated Marie-Antoinette.

There is the neo-classical Chapel of the Couvent de la Reine (1770) – now the Lycée Hoche – a little garden rotunda, and a few years later the delightful 'Normandy' farmhouse, dairy, and mill known as Le Hameau. There is something playfully Rococo about this artificial and, in retrospect, somewhat pathetic conception; but its real affinities are with the Picturesque movement which was affecting France at this time through the fashion for the 'natural' *jardin anglais*. It also shows a realization of the picturesque possibilities of vernacular architecture some time before the impulse which produced *cottages ornés* in England.

One example of an English garden (1780) separates Le Hameau from the Petit Trianon. Though its effects are in fact very carefully studied, its appearance of an irregular undulating landscape contrasts greatly with the formal straight-line garden of the seventeenth century. Its love of serpentine lines is suggestive of Rococo, while its Romanticism is also contrary to the rational Classicism of the earlier tradition. Follies and garden buildings were features of these conceptions, deriving no doubt from the temples which appeared in the landscape paintings of the Roman Campagna by Claude; but in addition to classical features such as Mique's cupolaed Temple de l'Amour and exquisite Belvédère octagonal, with its decoration in the Pompeian manner, at Versailles, and the less successful tall, 'classical' pagoda at Chanteloup, near Amboise, there were many other features such as Gothick ruins,

13. The Chapel, Versailles (1699): a grand Classical Baroque scheme, well-lit with decorative elements subordinate to clarity and reason. The exterior is more exuberant but with unexpected echoes of Gothic in its tall proportions, clerestory, and roof.

14a. Hôtel des Invalides (1671): a superb if somewhat severe design by Bruant. The rather bleak solemnity of the façades of the cour d'honneur is relieved by the ornamental trophies of the dormer windows and by Hardouin-Mansart's Dôme rising majestically behind.

14b. Place Stanislas, Nancy: fountains with leaden statues and wrought iron screen by Jean Lamour. Exquisite eighteenth-century street furnishings with all the light animated qualities of Rococo. The virtuosity of the technique matches the artistic excellence.

TEMPLE DE L'AMOUR, VERSAILLES

Chinese bridges – oriental exoticism again – and *cottages ornés*. The most prominent designer of such landscape compositions was François-Joseph Bélanger, who laid out the jardin *anglo-chinois* of the Folie St.-James, Neuilly, and the garden of the neo-classical Bagatelle in the Bois de Boulogne in the last quarter of the eighteenth century. Regrettably, there are few of these gardens left in France.

Besides his contributions to Versailles A. J. Gabriel's other major work is the finely planned École Militaire (1751), an angular, soberly restrained group of buildings comparable to the Invalides marking an evolutionary stage in the planning of public building complexes. Clearly articulated and very practical it took over twenty years to build; he was assisted by Brongniart, whose name will crop up again later on his own account. The Champ-de-Mars façade with its centre pavilion and four-sided dome has had its proportions affected by being lengthened by later blocks, but the façade to the great court is unspoilt. There are the two super-imposed colonnades of the Invalides in the main block, two lower wings, with the other side of the court left open. Special features are the Marshall's Hall, the chapel, and the staircase.

Gabriel's other monumental buildings in Paris are the Ministère de la Marine (1757) and the corresponding block – the Hôtel Crillon – on the other side of his rue Royale, both with façades which echo the colonnade of Perrault's Louvre, though the grand planning conception is Baroque.

M

In urban design Gabriel continued the line of development from his father but elaborated it. Thus the latter's square at Rennes (1721) – he also designed the Hôtel de Ville there – is a rectangle one side of which is taken up by a previous building, Salmon de Brosse's Palais de Justice. The other three are classical façades with a giant Ionic order over a basement. One side of J. J. Gabriel's Palace Royale (now Place de la Bourse) at Bordeaux (1731), however, is occupied by the river, anticipating the more open and less introverted approach of the later eighteenth century. The façades are decked with elegant Ionic columns and crowned with high unclassical French roofs. In contrast, his son's Place Louis v, Paris (1753), now the Place de la Concorde, has façades which are both more solemn and strictly classical, with a diminished basement, colossal order of Corinthian columns, and balustrades recalling Perrault's Louvre. But again one side is open to the river and it is flanked by the Champs-Élysées woods and the Tuileries gardens – Picturesque elements again – so that only the north side consists of architecture. This is a far cry from the rigidly confined and fully urban Italian Renaissance piazza. Its centre, as planned, with an equestrian monument surrounded by a dry moat bridged at several points made it even more original. (The syenite Egyptian obelisk of Rameses II is an addition of 1836.) Moreover, it is not a self-sufficient unit any more but related to the rue Royale with its terminating focus at the top, the church of the Madeleine. Altogether it was a brilliant conception and set a new standard of excellence.

These works of classical town planning executed in Louis xv's reign were of course in the tradition of royal squares already well established in France. The last and most perfectly classical is the Place Royale, Reims (1756) by Legendre, effectively related to the larger urban matrix and joined to the town hall by the great rue Colbert. The unfinished Place des Quinconces, Bordeaux, would have undoubtedly been most magnificent with its arched street entrances and handsome frontages, worthy of the Théâtre, by the same architect Victor Louis, and the many fine hôtels (including the present town hall and the Hôtel Labottière) and the curving line of paired houses along the Quai Richelieu with fine doorways, curved *entresols*, and windows with wrought iron balconies.

Before taking leave of the royal squares it is worth remarking on the considerable inventiveness with which French architects

HÔTEL LABOTTIÈRE

combined the basic horizontal divisions of their façades: ground floor basement, two living storeys, and roof with dormers. The proportions of these are varied to taste, so that in the Place Dauphine (1606), Paris, the two living storeys are equal, in the Place Vendôme they become an enlarged *bel étage* (piano nobile) and attic, and finally in the Place de la Concorde they are united by a colonnade and the entablature takes the place of the dormers, since the roof is now flat. The classical language is much more flexible than its critics would suggest, as these variations indicate.

Eighteenth-century hôtels de ville are usually unexceptional, though showing more ornament than those of the previous century. Such are Noyers, Avallon, and Saulieu. But others are large, majestic, and ennobled with classical orders. Often the grander designs are conceived in relation to some large square, such as J. J. Gabriel's building at Rennes (1744) which occupies one side of such a space: broad, well-proportioned with a three-storey classical façade reflecting basement, *bel étage*, and attic. Other examples are Beauvais (1752) and Metz (1766), by F. Blondel, on the side of the new Place d'Armes away from the cathedral. Toulouse (1760) is another example.

Among exchanges, outstanding are Soufflot's Loge des Changes, Lyon (1747) and Brongniart's Bourse des Valeurs, Paris (1808) in the First Empire manner of a large Corinthian temple whose magnificence takes precedence over utility in planning.

In the rebuilding of the Halle aux Blés after a disastrous fire in 1802, Bélanger used – surprisingly, for he was a landscape gardener, a neo-classicist and one of the inventors of the Empire style – an iron frame to support a roof made of sheets of copper plated with tin, an early instance of the use of iron architecturally in France. But this was a utilitarian job and did not represent, therefore, a full acceptance of the new material now available. That was to come a good deal later in the nineteenth century.

Eighteenth-century hospitals show a continuance of the earlier plan types already described, modified by styling of the period, e.g. Cochin Hospital (1780), the Charité by Antoine – with Doric portal – and the Beaujon Hospital (1784).

Ecclesiastical architecture of the eighteenth century saw the replacement of the church with aisles entirely by those of centralized and basilican plans. Of the basilican type the cathedral of Nancy (1706) by J. H. Mansart and Boffrand, already referred to, is a fine example, and other notable ones are Versailles Cathedral by Hardouin-Mansart's grandson, also mentioned; Arras Cathedral (c. 1755) by Pierre Constant d'Ivry; and the Madeleine, Besançon (1746) by Nicole. The Oratory at Avignon (1717) is in the first group and is elliptical, but the greatest of them all is the Panthéon, called until the Revolution Sainte-Geneviève, begun by Soufflot in 1757.

After that of Gabriel the name of Jacques-Germain Soufflot is the most eminent in later eighteenth-century French architecture. A pupil of Servandoni, his inclination was neo-classical, and in his efforts to recover some of the seriousness and correctness of earlier classical architecture he had looked both at Wren's work in England as well as at earlier examples in Rome itself.

The Panthéon, standing proudly at the top of its street, is

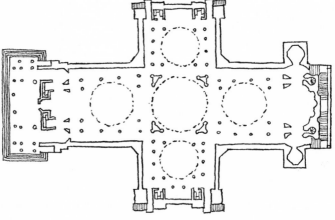

THE PANTHÉON, PARIS

Soufflot's most famous work. The plan is a Greek cross with all its arms aisled but without their being filled in. The walls are unbroken by openings, as the large clerestory windows cannot be seen externally, and their only ornamental feature is a continuous entablature decorated with festoons. There is a high, graceful, rather Baroque central dome – triple like that of the Invalides, but the outer one of stone – with a tall colonnaded drum over the crossing. Its debt to St. Paul's shows Wren's influence. There are also four lower domes, one over each arm, to give yet another variation of the five-domed scheme going back to Byzantium.

There is an interesting comparison to be made with Saint-Louis-des-Invalides. The portico of the Panthéon is not stepped back and the walls are plain and not articulated; the dynamism has gone. Here is the difference between Baroque and neo-classicism.

The neo-classicism of the later eighteenth century favoured colossal orders, and Soufflot's original contribution here was to support the domes not on pilastered piers as the Rococo had favoured but largely on columns. They had to be replaced by Rondelet's heavier piers eventually, but this use of Corinthian columns (with straight entablatures in the Panthéon) structurally

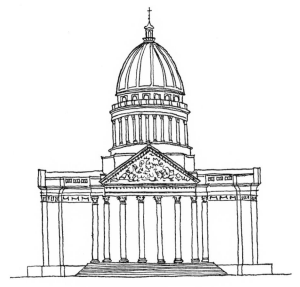

THE PANTHÉON, PARIS

in arcades, instead of the square pier usual in the seventeenth century, was a feature of eighteenth-century classical churches. They can be seen so used with round arches at Nancy and with a straight entablature at Arras. Windows are round-headed as a rule. The elegant interior of the Panthéon has both a Roman monumentality and a new regularity, the former quality leavened by a feeling of lightness that inevitably recalls Adam's style in Britain. But Soufflot supported his lightness and use of the column by a rational argument which appealed to Gothic structural theory; he had obviously remembered the structural function of the column in medieval architecture in his design. Adam's, on the other hand, was purely an aesthetic preference. Opposite the Panthéon, Soufflot did the École de Droit (1756). His other works include, in Lyons, the Hôtel-Dieu (1741), by which he made his name, the Loge de Changes (1747) and the hospital at Mâcon (1770); and in ecclesiastical architecture the church of the Visitation, Le Mans, and the Sacristy, Notre-Dame, Paris.

Soufflot was remarkable for his early admiration of Gothic architecture for its functional logic rather than for its emotive and associational qualities, as was the case with 'Gothick' in England, already in the grip of Romanticism. His was clearly a French response, just as that of Horace Walpole's is explicable in terms of a national predilection for tradition and literary values.

The Panthéon has a fine hexastyle portico façade, but Nancy, Arras, and St-Eustache, Paris, show the way in which eighteenth-century churches developed the two-tower façade of the medieval and Baroque periods. In the first half of the eighteenth century Saint-Sulpice was given a front which combined both the two-tower and the portico motifs. The work of the Florentine, Giovanni Servandoni, it was said to be 'in the manner of Palladio'. Its special niche in architectural history is that it represented in the 1730's one of the earliest reactions against Rococo in the direction of a stricter classicism.

As we have already observed, eighteenth-century churches were generally less restrained than those of the seventeenth century and partook of the elegant decoration of the Rococo. Exceptionally rich is some of the work in the cathedral at Nancy, and particularly the vivacious Bon-Secours chapel for Stanislas Leczinsky, where painting, carving, stucco work, and wrought iron afford a fine integrated display of the best French craftsmanship of the period.

SAINT-SULPICE, PARIS

Of monastic buildings of the earlier part of this century, those of the famous Abbaye-aux-Hommes, Caen, remodelled in 1704 by Père Guillaume de la Tremblaye round three courts, one the cloister court with Tuscan pilasters, exhibit what is now a feature of classically conceived convents, an important staircase, here with fine wrought iron work again.

The rationalism, however, that lay behind the enthusiasm for neo-classicism was fostered and spread during the eighteenth century by a large number of architectural writings. It began with the Abbé de Cordemoy's *Nouveau Traité de toute l'Architecture* (1706) but reached its apogee in M. A. Laugier's *Essai sur l'Architecture* (1753). Laugier was a Jesuit writer who, on the basis of the functional origins of architecture, propounded a rationalist theory of neo-classicism that proved very influential: with Soufflot for example. Three years after the publication of the *Essai* began the building of the Panthéon, the first great work of neo-classicism. The conjunction of dates is not accidental, and Laugier called it 'the first example of a perfect architecture'.

Soufflot had admired, besides Gothic architecture, the Greek temples he had seen and drawn in southern Italy; though he never adopted a neo-Greek style. The preference for Greek models, especially Doric, came in the reign of Louis XVI, when the ruins at Paestum became better known generally among architects and connoisseurs. There were, too, other currents coming together at this time to form a neo-classical stream more radical than the neo-classicism of A.-J. Gabriel's, lasting from *c.* 1775 to *c.* 1840, when it largely dispersed into other forms of revivalism – among them the influence of England, already noted, and the stimulus of the discoveries of late Roman Hellenic cities of Pompeii and Herculaneum.

Plans followed Early Christian basilicas and many of the decorative motifs were Etruscan in origin. Saint-Philippe-du-Roule, Paris (1774) by Jean-François Chalgrin, is such a simple rectangular timber-ceiled basilica (the first to reintroduce the plan), with a pedimented Doric portico. A more severe unaisled but double-apsed basilica is Saint-Louis-d'Antin (1781) by Alexandre-Théodore Brongniart, once the chapel of a Capuchin friary. The cloister of the latter, now the courtyard of the Lycée Condorcet, is part of an interesting example of late eighteenth-century monastic architecture: severely correct Doric with a Doric portico too.

These neo-classical churches were the first of a series extending well into the nineteenth century. Saint-Louis, Toulon (1782) resembles Saint-Philippe-du-Roule, and in Paris the best are Notre-Dame-de-Lorette (1823) by Le Bas, and Saint-Vincent-de-Paul (1824) by Lepère and Hittorf where Classical Revival has begun to make itself felt. 'Neo Classical', 'Romantic Classical', 'Classical Revival': one must always remember that a tradition does not remain the same but is subject to innovation, unconscious or not. Marx, it has been said, was not a Marxist and these French 'Classical' architects, however much they professed to keep close to their sources, inevitably brought about modifications that are of their own time and no other.

But in the following the developments in classical ecclesiastical architecture from the later eighteenth century onwards, we are running on too far, by-passing the work of an earlier generation and other manifestations of the neo-classical and in particular the Néo-Grec spirit. We must now, therefore, return to those architects who in France were the immediate followers of Gabriel and Soufflot. As a group they owed much to these two but also much to their own knowledge, acquired directly or indirectly from Rome through the Académie de France there, from their awareness of English classicism, and from their enthusiasm for the designs of Giovanni Battista Piranesi, the Venetian etcher of vast fantastic classical buildings cyclopean and rusticated which stimulated their imaginations. The result of these influences was a Romantic Classical mode, especially in the ideas of Marie-Joseph Peyre, one of the architects of the Odéon (1779) and later of Étienne-Louis Boullée, both of whom published in their turn influential designs of impressive but somewhat megalomaniac schemes.

Abstraction and a vast monumentality are in fact typical of the many drawings submitted in the period 1770–90 for the Prix de Rome, remarkable and highly imaginative designs, though never likely to have been built as planned. Their abstract geometrical qualities, which are classical, are coupled, however, with expressive personal feeling which Boullée the Romantic-Classicist advocated in his writings. He built remarkably little, some of the few works by his hand being the Hôtel Alexandre (1766), the Hôtel Brunoy (1772), both in Paris, and châteaux at Chaville, Montmorency, and Nogent-sur-Marne. The Hôtel de Salm by Pierre Rousseau, now the Chancellerie de la Légion D'Honneur dates from a decade later than Brunoy.

The Académie d'Architecture was suppressed in 1793 by the Convention and replaced by the Académie des Beaux-Arts, which helped to widen the gap between architectural design and practical building technology which the former had preserved, despite exceptions. Here, then, in these Prix de Rome drawings, is the origin of the Beaux-Arts tradition of abstract symmetrical planning which put aesthetics before functional requirements.

The style of this period, as well as its insistence on archaeological purity of detail, is typified by a use of geometrical forms – as we have seen, a contrast with the curves of Rococo – large plain wall surfaces, flat, concealed roofs, hemi-spherical Roman domes, coffered barrel-vaults, and porticos, usually Doric, Tuscan or Greek, with straight entablatures. Generally a short, thick-set version of the Tuscan order was preferred by the group of architects whose work we are discussing, but the original Greek Doric first appeared in France inside the massive cubic Théâtre, Besançon (1778) by Claude-Nicolas Ledoux. Here the auditorium is a strict hemicycle, not a Baroque 'horseshoe', the exterior having an unpedimented Ionic portico.

Ledoux began as a neo-classicist producing a country house at Eaubonne just north of Paris (1762), then the Pavillon de Louveciennes for Mme du Barry in 1771; but he evolved as a Romantic-Classicist, as is apparent in his design for the Hôtel Thélusson, Paris (1780), which combined triumphal arch and landscaped garden in the English manner. As we shall see, he moved on to an even more remarkable and extreme form of Romantic-Classicism, where his spare geometry is infused with strong personal feeling. Like other early practitioners of this mode he endeavoured to make it *parlante* or symbolically expressive.

The modern theatre appears in France only after the middle of the eighteenth century. The earliest were part of a larger entity, such as Gabriel's admirable and important Opéra at Versailles (1753) with its more advantageous U-shape plan to the auditorium, good acoustics, and fine decoration of the period.

The first independent theatre was the Grand Théâtre, Bordeaux (1772), by Victor Louis. To the auditorium and stage he added a vestibule, foyer, and double-flighted staircase. There is a large Corinthian portico with straight entablature in Louis' rather 'florid' classicism. The period used this type of colonnade for all types of monumental buildings and it turns up repeatedly.

The Odéon (originally the Comédie-Française) by Marie-Joseph Peyre and Charles de Wailly (1779, rebuilt after a fire, 1807) is a more severe design. Also to the late seventies belong the semi-cylindrical theatre of Besançon by Ledoux – already mentioned – and those of Nantes by Crucy, and Amiens by Pierre Rousseau. The tendency was to reduce the classical portico to a façade or simply a portico of four columns, as in the Variétés (1807) and the Gymnase, later, both in Paris.

GRAND THÉÂTRE, BORDEAUX

Good work was done in the neighbourhood of Besançon about this time by P. A. Paris, notably the hôtel de ville at Neuchâtel and the hospital at Bourg-en-Bresse, carrying on the tradition of good provincial architecture such as that of Diviler and Giral in Montpellier of a century earlier and the work of Héré at Nancy, architecture that was not 'provincial' in any perjorative sense.

Though much has now gone, other good specimens of Ledoux's work are the hôtels d'Uzès and d'Hallwyl, Paris, of the sixties, the Hôtel de Montmorency and the plain, severely cubical Château de Bénouville, near Caen, of the seventies. The design of the Hôtel de Montmorency is originally planned on a diagonal axis and has oval and circular apartments. From the eighties date the barriers or toll houses of Paris, e.g. the Barrière de St. Martin, Place de Stalingrad (a cylinder on a prism) extraordinarily varied and powerful compositions of plain geometrical forms and rusticated columns of Tuscan or Doric such as are used in the Directors' Pavilion, the Salines de Chaux, Arc-et-Senans, near Besançon (1775). This is one of the earliest examples of industrial architecture in France. In the entrance portico to the salt pits, Doric – again with straight entablature rather than a pediment – combines an elemental neo-classicism with romantic rock-like rustication so that the two main cultural forces of the time are seen in confluence. The union shows too, clearly, that Ledoux was not content

BARRIÈRE DE SAINT-MARTIN, PARIS

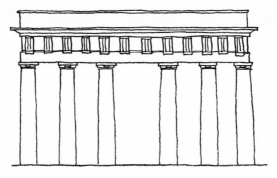

PORTICO, ARC-ET-SENANS

with mere imitations of Greek or Renaissance architecture but how he sought to use their forms freely to express his own ideas and to serve the new needs of his own time, as David did in painting.

Ledoux also published a scheme for an ideal city of Chaux in 1804, interestingly original but full of rather grandiose rhetoric that, as we have seen, would appear to stem in part at least from Piranesi's, but mostly from his own dreams of gigantic geometry.

With Boullée, Ledoux is now recognized as one of the chief originators in France of Romantic Classicism, a syncretic style that took in a good deal more than classical revival, and owed much to the earlier theorizing of Langier.

Other works of this phase of French architecture by architects whose reputations were greater in their day than Ledoux's include J. A. Antoine's splendid Hôtel de la Monnaie (the Mint), Paris (1768), infused with Roman *gravitas* – though he never went to Rome and as a neo-classicist he gave the chapel of the Charité, already mentioned, a Greek Doric peristyle – and Jacques Gondoin's École de Médecine (1769), with its functional plan, dissecting theatre, and echoes of Rome in its Corinthian portico and Colosseum-like entrances. The theatre here was very advanced for its time and was the prototype, for example, of the hemicyclical Salle des Cinq-Cents of the Chamber of Deputies, in the old Palais-Bourbon, first adapted in 1795. Brongniart's Lycée Condorcet (1781) has also been referred to already, and his career, as we have seen, extended into the Empire period, for in 1808 he built the Paris Bourse with its lofty Corinthian columns, later enlarged. Generally, however, there was for political and financial

reasons very little executed architecture in France between the
Revolution and 1806; though designing went on. After 1806
came a great outburst of First Empire building activity.

Like Ledoux and Gondoin, Jean Chalgrin, a pupil of Boullée,
was much taken by Greek proportions. But the architect of Saint-
Philippe-du-Roule (1774) is better known for his posthumous Arc
de Triomphe de l'Étoile, not completed until 1835. Commemorat-
ing Napoleon's great victories and as such a potent symbol of
la gloire, it has since become the most important single focus of
patriotic feeling among Frenchmen. The sculptural decoration
is later than Chalgrin and heavier in style, but in any case, compared with the late eighteenth century the style associated with
the Empire reveals a tendency towards the relaxation of geometrical rigidity and severity of line, and a growing grandeur
and ornateness exemplified by La Madeleine. This was originally
conceived in 1806 by Pierre Vignon as a memorial temple to the
soldiers of Napoleon's Grande Armée, and was continued by
Huvé in 1828 but not finished until 1842. Externally it is an
octostyle peripteral Roman Corinthian temple standing on a high
podium, which, together with its 'island' site, effectively isolates
it and makes it more imposing. Its monumental portico with pediment the sculptured tympanum by Lemaire depicting the Last

LA MADELEINE, PARIS

Judgement – is thus reached up a long flight of wide steps, and its magnificent 'cella' nave has no windows, being top-lit from its three saucer domes, one over each bay, and a semi-dome over the apse. Of structural interest is the fact that the entablature is constructed not of flat lintels but of voussoirs; of stylistic interest is its 'funereal' Romantic Classical interior; and of town-planning interest is its effectiveness as an urban focus. The precedent is again Roman rather than Greek, though the internal domes are not apparent externally, as is also apparent from Gondoin's Imperial column in the Place Vendôme made from the bronze of captured cannon. Another design of the Empire period is B. Poyet's front of the Chambre des Députés (1807), a projecting dodecastyle pedimented portico above a broad flight of steps flanked by severe rusticated wings without openings. Once more the tone is of sternness and grandeur; the fidelity to Roman precedent is unmistakable.

The beautiful Arc du Carrousel (1806) with its bronze quadriga above was designed to provide an imposing entrance arch to the Palais des Tuileries, where Charles Percier and Pierre Fontaine carried out alterations for Napoleon as well as at the architecturally restrained Malmaison (1802) – where their characteristic decorative style is well-displayed in the Library and Josephine's

ARC DU CARROUSEL, PARIS

CHÂTEAU DE MALMAISON

tent-like bedroom – the Louvre, and other royal residences. It is not without significance that these two pupils of Peyre were introduced to the Emperor by David, the severely classical painter; they became the leading exponents of the Empire style in architecture and decoration and the founders of what later became famous as the École des Beaux-Arts, founded in 1816 as a state institution and in that sense a continuation of the Académie.

Percier and Fontaine, however, were not inseparable, and it was the former, assistant to Chalgrin, who restored the Palais-Royal and built the Hôtel-Dieu, Pontoise (1823), while Fontaine was responsible at the Restoration for the somewhat severe but exquisite Chapelle Expiatoire, Paris (1816), in memory of the dead king and queen. Its refined centralized chapel has an entrance portico, apses on three sides and a dome which, like so many of the period, not only in France, owes much to the Roman Pantheon. With its galleries and vestibules it forms a most harmonious composition in the Romantic Classical mode, showing how it not only continued, strengthened, into the Empire period but survived it.

Not a great many châteaux had been built during the last quarter of the eighteenth century even before the Revolution broke but in the Loire valley, where it makes an instructive contrast with earlier examples, Montgeoffroy (1775), with its contemporary furnishings, illustrates the grace and refinement that was one aspect of the late eighteenth century; though it still retains elegant versions of the tall roofs, chimneys, and dormer windows associated with the earlier period of French domestic architecture.

There is no space to deal with the numerous bridges of Paris

CHÂTEAU DE MONTGEOFFROY

but if the Pont Neuf is the oldest and the late eighteenth-century Pont Royale is the most beautiful with its elegant arches and sensitive proportions, mention must be made of the Pont de la Concorde, a splendidly dignified work – considerably widened since it was built in 1787 – by Jean Perronet who was one of the first to apply in the spirit of the time, scientific analysis to the problems of constructing masonry bridges, thus achieving greater and more graceful spans. Also in the spirit of the age was the use of cast iron for the first time in the Pont des Arts (1803) and the Pont d'Austerlitz (1806). From the late nineteenth century is the most ornate bridge, the Pont Alexandre III with its single metal span, columns, and sculptures.

Since the later seventeenth century in the time of Louis XIV French architects had carried French ideas in architecture and decoration into Northern and Central Europe: Le Blond in St Petersburg, the La Vallées in Stockholm with perhaps François Cuvilliés as the most outstanding example with his Rococo masterpiece, the Amalienburg at Nymphenburg, Munich, Bavaria (1734). Now the political dominance of Napoleon again enhanced the prestige of French architectural ideas elsewhere in Europe. They had become particularly influential in Italy since the emergence of neo-Classicism about the middle of the eighteenth century and were to continue to exert a powerful attraction on that country throughout the nineteenth century despite her own strong indigenous classical tradition.

Both before and after the Empire, America was also affected by developments in France from L'Enfant's plan for Washington,

15a. Hôtel de Ville, Paris: original design 1837, rebuilt 1876. The nineteenth century was an era of Revivalism in architecture and this handsome new town hall sought in a picturesque way to recapture the extravagance of the Early Renaissance.

15b. The Bourse, Paris (1808): Brongniart's great square 'temple' without a pediment is in the lofty Roman manner associated with the public architecture of the Empire period. The primary aim was an impressive exterior, but the functional needs within are not neglected.

16a. Marseille: Le Corbusier's Unité d'Habitation (1952) has a bold façade with deeply recessed cellular openings that cleverly scale down its seventeen storeys. The midway shopping level with *brise-soleil* provides an effective horizontal accent.

16b. Royan: heavily bombed in World War II the town has many new buildings including this Protestant church with its contemporary bell-tower and 'atrium'.

D.C. (1791) – emanating ultimately from conceptions like Versailles – to Hunt's French Renaissance and Richardson's Neo-Romanesque beginning in the 1850's and 1870's respectively. Neo-Grecians like Jefferson, however, owed quite as much to English examples, and Latrobe, himself from England, was a pupil of Charles Cockerell.

Some of the major influential French treatises on architecture have already been alluded to. One type of publication going back to the late seventeenth century consisted of courses of lectures, and of these the most seminal in the eighteenth and nineteenth centuries were those of Jacques François Blondel, published in the 1770's, and J. N. L. Durand's *Leçons* (1802), which sum up French architectural education of the period. Durand was a pupil of Boullée who taught at Napoleon's École Polytechnique and his treatise was one of the most important of the Empire period. An advocate of rationalism in architecture, he produced theories that have proved attractive even to twentieth-century architects, thus providing an ideological link between the neo-classicists of the eighteenth century and the modern movement.

CHAPTER EIGHT

The Nineteenth Century

T HE period which followed the passing of the First Empire began with a continuation of the established, rather cold, dry, severe Romantic Classical mode (by now an international style, if mainly French in origin), as in the fine Saint-Denis-du-Saint-Sacrement, Paris (1823), an elegant barrel-vaulted basilica in the tradition of Saint-Philippe-de-Roule and Notre-Dame-de-Lorette of the same vintage. By Hippolyte Le Bas, who had collaborated with Brongniart on the Bourse, the latter is a five-aisled Early Christian basilica with classical features such as portico and domed chancel, i.e. an eclectic Romantic Classical design.

But though there was nothing in French architecture to correspond to the innovations of Delacroix and Géricault in painting, what was to be the characteristic theme of nineteenth-century architecture – historicism – became increasingly perceptible, and architects who once were content to work mainly in what was the particular form of classicism favoured in their time widened their horizons and looked further afield for inspiration.

We have already noted a revived interest in Early Christian architecture in Notre-Dame-de-Lorette, but the splendid church of Saint-Vincent-de-Paul, Paris (1824), by J. B. Lepère and the German-born Jakob Hittorf, also a five-aisled basilica, is a classical design with a two-towered façade, following Percier and Fontaine in some ways, that has a rich interior and an open timber roof clearly inspired by Early Christian basilicas. Another feature now lost was the polychrome effects of the exterior; it was Hittorf who discovered the polychromy of antique Greek architecture (1830), much to the discomfiture of the purists.

However, what is more to our immediate point is that there is also detectable in the exterior a new leaning towards the Italian Renaissance. Percier and Fontaine played a part in preparing for the Classical Revival in the nineteenth century by publishing their important works on the historical buildings of Rome, and, as we have seen, some of the designs of Ledoux's contemporaries

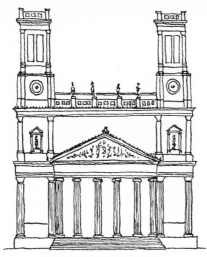

SAINT-VINCENT-DE-PAUL, PARIS

show not only Néo-Grec motifs but also a liking for Renaissance-looking columned loggias and arcades.

Yet the revival of the Italian Renaissance mode proper did not begin in France until the 1820's; before this the influence had been quite the other way round, as architecture in Italy had for a period clearly reflected French taste as a concomitant of the political dominance of France. Two examples are Charles Rohault de Fleury's heavily rusticated Italianate barracks in the rue Mouffetard (1827) and the fine Hôtel Pourtalès (1836) by F. L. J. Duban, who, preferring it to Antique architecture, became an authority on that of the Italian High Renaissance; though his later École des Beaux-Arts (1860) shows originality as well as a commendable restraint considering its Second Empire date.

Native sources, too, were not overlooked by the revivalists. Already in 1822 the so-called 'Maison de François I' had been built as part of an Early Renaissance design. In 1837 the Hôtel de Ville, Paris, was extended sympathetically by Godde and Lesueur in the same mode, later to be rebuilt by Ballu and Deperthes in 1876, with handsome high-roofed elevations.

In the 1840's both these strands of Renaissance Revival may be observed. J. Lacornée's Foreign Ministry on the Quai d'Orsay (1846), with its superimposed arch orders, is conceived in rich, somewhat Venetian terms, while the École Normale Supérieure

(1841) by Gisors is French Renaissance, yet looking forward to the Second Empire in its high mansard roofs that seem to be reintroduced for the first time here.

But these are not the only historicist strands in the fabric of French architecture by the fourth decade of the century. There was also Neo-Gothic. Deriving partly from the example of Britain, the style was never taken up in France to the extent which it was in its spiritual home, and it was chiefly confined to ecclesiastical architecture. Gothic had of course never really died out, as is shown by Orléans Cathedral rebuilt from the seventeenth to the nineteenth century, and by some Jesuit churches erected long after the Middle Ages had receded.

We saw how Soufflot admired its structural logic, ingenuity and boldness. The romantic medievalism of the eighteenth and early nineteenth century nourished it. Like Sir Walter Scott in Britain (and throughout Europe for that matter), Victor Hugo did much to stimulate interest in the Middle Ages in France and thus helped to prepare the ground for a revived form of Gothic architecture, which almost always in the nineteenth century carried literary overtones, despite the more rational approach of men like Viollet-le-Duc whom we shall shortly consider – the approach which stemmed from Laugier and Soufflot.

By the July Monarchy of Louis-Philippe (1830–48) Gothic revival was sufficiently established for F. C. Gau and Ballu to use it for the great church of Sainte-Clotilde (1846), an essay in fourteenth-century Rayonnant, though a contemporary of the classical church of Saint-Vincent-de-Paul. (Ballu was also capable of producing a Neo-Early Renaissance design as his large Trinité of 1861 shows.)

Other examples, apart from the Neo-Gothic façade added to the fifteenth-century church of Saint-Ouen, Rouen, in 1845, are the superbly sited Notre-Dame-de-Bon-Secours (1840), overlooking the same town, by J. E. Barthélémy; J. B. Lassus's rather stodgy Saint-Jean-de-Belleville, Paris (1854); and the large but not very effective Saint-Epvre, Nancy (1855) by M. P. Morey. Despite its cast iron structure which will be adverted to later, Saint-Augustin, Paris, in the sixties still found it necessary to assume a medieval appearance.

By then Neo-Gothic had passed its peak, which was reached with the Second Empire. Its dominant spirit from 1840 to 1870 was that of Eugène-Emmanuel Viollet-le-Duc, the man who did so much drastic restoration of medieval cathedrals and of Carcassonne and the Château de Pierrefonds, drastic because he sacrificed minor portions in different styles to the interest of a specious uniformity with the principal mode. The château of Coucy, the abbeys of Vézelay and Saint-Denis, Saint-Sernin, Toulouse, and Saint-Ouen, Rouen, are some of the other best-known scenes of his considerable activity in the field of restoration.

The realization of what had been lost by the vandalistic destruction of the great Romanesque work of the abbey of Cluny in 1810 and of the cloisters at Toulouse had already caused the Commission for Historical Monuments (1837) to be set up – Prosper Mérimée was an inspector – which initiated the restoration of Notre-Dame and Sainte-Chapelle. Viollet-le-Duc assisted at Notre-Dame where his chapter house (1847) is an admirable original design. Unfortunately, he did not himself build a great deal. One of his few churches is Saint-Denys-de-l'Estrée (1864), well above average for French Neo-Gothic work. Vaulted throughout, it has a rather complex exterior with western tower over the porch and a projecting Lady Chapel at the east end. The detailing is simple but effective.

Viollet-le-Duc also made a name for himself as a researcher and theorist producing a number of very influential books, notably his *Dictionnaire raisonné de l'architecture française* (1854) and his *Entretiens*, the first volume of which appeared in 1863. In the latter particularly, his importance lies in the way he encouraged architects to revive the basic architectural concern for structure which medieval builders had shown but which had been much neglected during the classical centuries. In this and his championship of iron frame building, which he likened in principle to Gothic, Viollet-le-Duc anticipated one aspect of the modern movement.

Gothic Revival, however, was not the only form of medievalism to which the romanticism of the nineteenth century harked back. Neo-Romanesque too had its advocates and practitioners. Examples of the mode in Paris include Saint-Ambroise (1863) by Ballu again, and Notre-Dame-des-Champs.

Dating from 1852 is the huge domed polychromatic cathedral of Marseille – the chief work of Léon Vaudoyer – in a sort of Byzantine-Romanesque, while Nîmes has C. A. Questel's large cruciform church of Saint-Paul (1876), an impressive design rib-vaulted throughout and with a fine central lantern.

The famous Sacré-Cœur, Montmartre (1874), with its pale

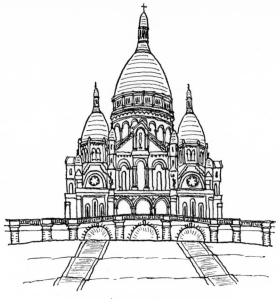

SACRÉ-CŒUR, PARIS

elevations and very prominent 'oriental' domes, may perhaps be best described as Romanesque-Byzantine, for which, as we have seen, there was some precedent earlier in the century in Marseille Cathedral and the church of Notre-Dame at Auteuil. Built as a votive offering after the disastrous Franco-Prussian War, Sacré-Cœur was inspired in part at least by Saint-Front, Périgueux, on which Abadie was working. The material is the dense limestone from Château-Landon, the same as that used for the Arc de Triomphe. Sacré-Cœur was completed by Lucien Magne.

Under Napoleon III Louis Visconti and later Hector-Martin Lefuel finally completed the Louvre and remodelled Du Cerceau's two-storey façade with pilasters and alternating triangular and segmental pediments, dating from Henri IV's time and intending to provide a link with the Tuileries. Thus – except that Louis XIV was mainly occupied with Versailles – the Louvre offers an epitome of the long period of French architecture from the reign of François I to the nineteenth century.

To the earlier contributions already described, Napoleon I had commissioned Percier and Fontaine, the architects of the splendid western part of the rue de Rivoli, to add a storey to the western half of the north and south sides of the court and a small portion at the north-east corner of the Place Louis-Napoléon. A little later, from 1806, they began the north wing from the Pavillon de Marsan to the Pavillon de Rohan to link up with the Tuileries.

It was to help to effect a satisfactory junction between the two royal palaces that Napoleon III ordered Visconti and Lefuel to build the New Louvre (1852) in an elaborate 'Neo-Baroque' style on the north and south of the Place Louis-Napoléon. Its main function was to provide administrative accommodation and a library, but its appearance was to be uniform and palatial with centre and corner pavilions with high mansard roofs, which, now revived, became one of the hall-marks of this new pompous eclectic Second Empire style – especially the curved types which appeared here over the central pavilions. From 1860 Lefuel refaced the Pavillons de Flore and de Marsan and the wings along the Seine and rue de Rivoli. Splendid nineteenth-century interiors are the Salle des Colonnes and the Salle d'Auguste.

The Second Empire mode, however, was not a 'revival' but a more sumptuous, more plastic modulation of earlier Renaissance Revival in the direction of Baroque: a rich and vigorous style that

NEW LOUVRE, CORNER PAVILION

expressed the extravagent assertive spirit of Napoleon III's reign. But in practice there was much stylistic variety.

Beginning in the time of Louis-Philippe but largely built under the Second Empire are the utilitarian Durandesque Hôtel-Dieu and the elaborate Palais de Justice, Paris. There is Duban's École des Beaux-Arts already referred to, and there is the work of Auguste Vaudremer, who in the early sixties produced not only the Santé Prison, Paris (1862), an essentially utilitarian if somewhat *Rundbogenstil* structure, a type of building characteristic of the period, but also the noble basilica of Saint-Pierre-de-Montrouge in a restrained version of Neo-Romanesque. But all these in varying degrees historicist works show how far the old academic form of classicism had been ousted by the middle of the nineteenth century; though classical dispositions in planning and massing even yet were very influential and monumental effects were still sought after, under the auspices of the École des Beaux-Arts. The latter, however, never encouraged the extremes to which some carried these tendencies.

The most symbolic single work of the Second Empire, a period which produced so many elaborate and even pretentious buildings, not only in France, is properly the National Academy of Music (1861), known as the Paris Opéra, by Charles Garnier.

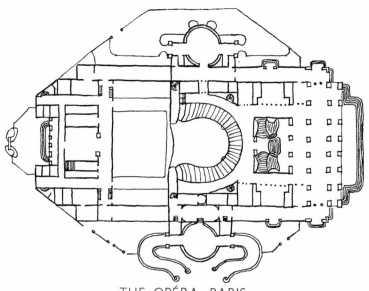

THE OPÉRA, PARIS

Here, given due prominence by Baron Haussmann's urban planning, is a very great development of Louis' plan for the Bordeaux theatre. The exterior design is no longer a rigid box-like form but one freely adapted to express the various elements that go to make up the very imaginatively planned Neo-Baroque composition, fully characteristic of the showy parvenue qualities of the period; though it was not in fact finished at the time of the Commune.

The façade is richly composed. Wide steps lead to a grand portico, the piers of which are embellished with symbolic figures of the arts. Large twinned columns with flanking subsidiary orders (Bramante and Michelangelo) and prominent balconies are features of the loggia, while the side pavilions were finished with segmental pediments reminiscent of Lescot's Louvre. The attic above is also sculptured with festoons and masks, while beyond is seen the low dome which marks the position of the auditoriums.

The contemporary liking for the ornate and sumptuous is even better seen in the lush interior decoration by Baudry and Carpeaux. It is an original mixture typical of the taste of that time gilt, bronze, Pyrenean marble, and porphyry in a luxuriant display of eclectic motifs and rich materials, Baroque and especially Venetian Renaissance, with obvious affinities with High Victorian work on this side of the Channel.

THE OPÉRA, PARIS

All this magnificent rhetoric makes it clear that this is not just a functional theatre but a lavish setting for public and social occasions. Hence the vast entrance hall, a great glittering foyer the width of the façade, with the Escalier d'Honneur, commanding it and running right from ground floor to top floor, and the large corridors. The boxes too are on an especially elaborate scale and there is a special Foyer de la Danse for season-ticket holders. Some might find the total effect altogether a little overblown; but the planning is superb and the exterior is an undeniably magnificent harmony of classical elements skilfully enriched and ornamented.

Garnier also built the famous Casino at Monte Carlo (1878), finely sited with a two-tower façade, so that the style became popular for gaming houses elsewhere and influenced the architecture of late nineteenth-century seaside resorts and spas. It was well-suited to their purpose and atmosphere. He also did the Casino and Baths at Vittel, and, in a less extravagant manner, the Nice Observatory.

The Palais Longchamp, Marseille (1862) by H. J. Espérandieu, who had built the bombastic Notre-Dame-de-la-Garde in the same city in 1854, is a more impressive neo-Baroque design: two museum blocks linked by a curved colonnade embracing a long cascade ending in a large spread of still water. The Place Henri Bergson and the hôtel de ville, Calais, are other examples of this phase of French architecture. Again, with Second Empire designs it is not easy to decide when panache becomes vulgar exhibitionism.

The principles of classical town planning which we have already seen operating in France in the seventeenth and eighteenth centuries were carried forward like French Classic architecture into the period of the First Empire, when Napoleon I tried to transform Paris into an Antique city with temples like the Madeleine and the Palais-Bourbon, columns and triumphal arches such as the Colonne de la Grand Armée and the Arc de Triomphe in the star-shaped Place d'Étoile, a motif which was prominent in the so-called Artists' Plan of 1797.

The Madeleine is significantly made the focus of the vista of the rue Royale, while the Arc de Triomphe is the focus of several radiating avenues. Percier and Fontaine's rue de Rivoli, five storeys with arcaded ground floor and dormered mansard roof, and the rue de Castiglione are among the best expressions of that tradition of uniform street architecture which can be traced back to *c.* 1600 and even to the rue Dauphine and the houses on the Pont Notre-Dame from a hundred years before that. Another such example is the rue de la Paix; while the polygonal Place Lafayette is a good example of the stately regularity of urban design in the twenties under the restored Bourbons.

What is new in the imperial schemes, however, is a willingness to pursue a ruthless policy of demolition in the desire to create great fresh vistas down wide avenues. It was a tendency that was most uncompromisingly adopted by Napoleon's administrator, Baron Haussmann, Préfet of the Seine Department. True, by his time the phenomenal growth and congestion of Paris required drastic action, but Haussmann's concern was not with traffic circulation particularly. He enlarged the obstructive Halles Centrales, the markets of central Paris, instead of removing them (not until the mid-twentieth century were they to be demolished and replaced by new markets near Orly and district shopping centres), and he neglected the approaches to the new important railway stations. He was very much concerned with aesthetic considerations and with minimizing the opportunities for civil disorder.

To prevent the latter he cleared the Île de la Cité of congested housing, opened up the main axes meeting at the 'Croisée de Paris' which became the Place du Châtelet, and made streets which were too wide and straight to be effectively blocked by barricades as they had been before. As things turned out Haussmann's drastic changes may have helped to provoke the rising of the Commune in 1871; he certainly did not prevent it by his work. In his efforts to achieve purely aesthetic effects he did things like making the boulevard Malesherbe lead nowhere, since its main function was to counterpoise the boulevard de la Madeleine.

To summarize the other principal ways in which the Baron left his mark on Paris: he completed the ring of boulevards which had been started on the line of the medieval walls (the medieval city had grown by a series of successively enlarged concentric walls, the abandoned inner ones thus becoming circulation roads), and greatly developed the outer system dating from the late eighteenth century. He created the three-mile straight stretch of the rue de La Fayette, and he implemented large scale lay-outs to the north-west, underpinned by the symmetrical crossroads of the Carrefours de la Madeleine and de l'Opéra (the grouping of the buildings defining the Place de l'Opéra gives it a

Neo-Baroque character matching that of the Opéra itself and very different from the 'classical' type of square), the Place du Trocadéro, and of course the Place de l'Étoile, the avenues of which he increased to twelve, while Hittorf regularized the neighbouring façades. By creating an exclusive district to the west he caused the well-to-do to leave the Marais and the Faubourg Saint-Antoine and thus drove a socially divisive wedge between the classes which before then had not been so sharply segregated.

Though Haussmann was dismissed in 1870 because of the controversy which his work produced, rigid and ruthless as it was, it was too late to undo it and to a substantial degree, therefore, the aspect of modern Paris – for better or for worse – is due to him.

The great parks of the Bois de Vincennes and the Bois de Boulogne laid out under Napoleon III are extensions into the nineteenth century of the landscaped 'English garden' ideas, by which the Picturesque made such a valuable contribution to the townscape of the large urban community.

Though France is a country of few large cities most of its urban expansion dates from the nineteenth century, which still dominates the face of most provincial towns which chiefly endeavoured to reflect the aspect of Paris in their central areas. From the second half of the century Marseille, which grew to its present size after the opening of the Suez Canal and the founding of a Colonial empire in North Africa, has the Canebière – its business centre and symbol of its prosperity – focusing on the church of Saint-Vincent-de-Paul at the top and continuing along the boulevard de la Libération. One of the best buildings of the period is the Exchange (1842) by M. R. Penchaud, in its own stuccoed place, but the columned Chamber of Commerce near the Old Port is also representative. The great harbour on which the trade of Marseille is dependent has been rebuilt since the Second World War.

To return now to Paris: some of the best of the mostly not greatly distinguished apartment houses put up in such great numbers during the nineteenth century to accommodate the rapidly growing population are those of Charles Garnier, with considerably improved planning behind their conservative eclectic façades; they include the first modern luxury flats in Paris. The standard arrangement of the apartment house (itself so characteristic an expression of French social life) is round an inner court or well with a central entrance and porter's lodge giving access to the stairs.

15 rue de Douai (*c.* 1860) is a block by Viollet-le-Duc mildly Gothic, though he usually preferred a Second Empire eclecticism for his secular work. It is neatly accommodated to its neighbours in what is the more usual mode of the period. In the Place de la Madeleine may be seen a house with a Neo-Gothic lower half, a Classic upper half, and a mansard roof with dormer windows. 11 rue de Milan (*c.* 1860) by A. F. Mortier, on the other hand, has a busy and vigorous Neo-Baroque façade. Despite these stylistic variations, however, a sensible building code ensured that a general consonance was maintained in the main design whatever the detailing. Where further height was required, for example, storeys had to be stepped back or mansards with attics introduced.

Lefuel's work at the Louvre, despite innovations of style, was still along traditional lines, but already there had been portents of a new kind of architecture. The rationalism from the eighteenth century and the emphasis on structural logic by Viollet-le-Duc have been mentioned. Besides these ideas, and also well-regarded by Viollet-le-Duc, were new materials.

Iron had been used in the roof of the Grand Théâtre, Bordeaux (1772), and with glass (another new material when used in this way, constructionally) it was employed in the dome of the Halle aux Blés (1805), a French invention of F. J. Bélanger, whom we have met previously as the designer of 'English' gardens and one of the founders of the Empire style.

But the question of the architectural use of iron was still controversial in 1842, as the business of reconstructing the Halles Centrales shows. Under Louis-Philippe, Baltard had devised a plan to be executed in stone, but after 1853 Napoleon III made him and Haussmann accept iron on the recommendation of the engineer Horeau, who had pioneered the new material and who, incidentally, submitted a ferrovitreous design for our own Great Exhibition (1851), before Paxton's 'Crystal Palace'. The result at the Halles Centrales was good functional planning and a somewhat traditionalist use by Baltard of cast iron columns and wrought iron roof trusses.

The central markets at Lyon received their iron roof in 1858. Here thirty years earlier Baltard had built his enormous Government Warehouse, an exceptional example of a nineteenth-century building of a functional nature conceived in classical terms.

The iron and glass train sheds of the great terminus stations are a typical application of the new technology and the results are magnificent in their own way. Among them was that of the Gare de l'Est – since replaced – by Baltard again. The main building (1847) by F. A. Duquesney is in an Italian Renaissance manner with a long loggia linking two blocks on either side of the great arched shed.

Hittorf, too, though capable of the grand classical rhetoric of the Gare du Nord (1861) in a Beaux-Arts style, also showed himself interested in the new materials of iron and glass ever since he had worked with Bélanger on Les Halles.

One of the first buildings where iron was used on a large scale was Henri Labrouste's Bibliothèque Sainte-Geneviève, Paris (1843), where it is employed both with feeling and intelli-

BIBLIOTHÈQUE NATIONALE, PARIS

gence for slender columns and vaulting arches, the lower parts of which are hidden inside the astylar Neo-Renaissance stone building, which is itself a fine strong design, elegantly and originally detailed. This amounts to an ingenious use of the new matarial within the context of a traditional design. Both his use of iron and his restrained classicism show Labrouste as essentially a rationalist.

This was the first separately-built library in France, and Labrouste also built additions to the Bibliothèque Nationale in 1862, where he made further structural advances in the use of iron and achieved remarkable effects of lightness and elegance, particularly in the many-domed reading room and strikingly 'modern' Magasin, or stacks, next to it.

Less than a decade later than the Sainte-Geneviève library, iron was used for the entire interior of Saint-Eugène, Paris (1854) by L. A. Boileau. Sainte-Clotilde had had an iron roof, and above the vaults of Chartres Cathedral, as far back as 1837, iron had been used for practical purposes. Here at Saint-Eugène, arcades and rib vault were constructed of iron, without Gothic decoration, despite the objections of academic architects, who were not interested in the full range of possibilities being opened up by developments in engineering and technology.

Baltard's domed basilica of Saint-Augustin, Paris (1860), was one of the first iron-framed churches in France, though less consistent than Saint-Eugène and, retrogressively, the iron work is treated like stone. Moreover, a good deal of the detailing is also in the new material. The cast iron structure, however, has been 'architecturally' clothed in stone façades in a Romanesque–Gothic mode kept distinct from the 'engineering'. The desire for a worthy façade, while at the same time using new techniques of construction, reflects the largely opposing views of the Académie des Beaux-Arts and the École Polytechnique and was paralleled elsewhere in Western Europe at this time.

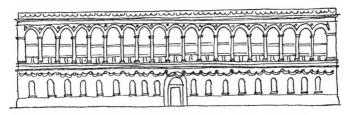

BIBLIOTHÈQUE SAINTE-GENEVIÈVE, PARIS

It was left to Jules Saulnier to devise the first complete iron frame building with mere coloured wooden tiles as infilling for the walls in the Chocolate Factory (1871) for Menier's at Noisiel-sur-Marne, near Paris. Its origin owed much to Viollet-le-Duc's early appreciation of the structural effectiveness of the Gothic system and his proselytizing on behalf of iron.

Another commercial work of the seventies in which iron figured importantly is the Bon Marché (1876) by Boileau *fils* – that characteristic building of modern urban societies, the large department store, had begun its career in earnest with the rise of middle-class affluence during the Second Empire. The metal and glass interior of the Bon Marché is now clothed in a masonry façade of the 1920's.

Iron and glass together were used in the roofs of *galeries* and *passages* – rows or arcades of covered shops – which became so characteristic a feature of the nineteenth-century urban scene. Paris was particularly rich in examples but the finest surviving early specimen is in Nantes, the three-storey Passage Pommeraye (1843) by Durand-Gasselin and J. B. Buron.

From 1855 the various International Expositions of the second half of the nineteenth century, though temporary affairs of short duration in themselves, did much to stimulate fresh thought in building and to provide opportunities for experimental work and a stage for its display. This 'laboratory' function of great exhibitions is one that we have become very familiar with and serves a most useful purpose when the inevitable frivolities have been discarded.

Cast iron and, after 1855 when Bessemer's converter process had cheapened their production, steel structures – vast halls enclosing large areas – were a particular feature of nineteenth-century French expositions. The 1867 exposition was almost entirely constructed of iron, while that of 1889 produced the pioneer light and airy, steel and glass Galerie des Machines (engineer: Cottancin), now demolished, which made the notable technical achievement of a span of 380 feet with its giant arches. The exposition, however, is better known for the Tower nearly 1,000 feet high built on the Champ-de-Mars by Gustave Eiffel, the engineer of the famous Garabit railway viaduct (1880), over the Truyère, who had collaborated with Garnier on the Nice Observatory and with Boileau on the Bon Marché and had done an important glass and iron entrance building for the Exposition of

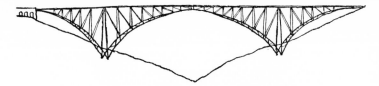

VIAUR BRIDGE, AVEYRON

1878. In the same year as the Garabit Viaduct, Eiffel began the first steel bridge in France, the Viaur railway bridge, Aveyron. This was a steel-arch deck-bridge with a main span of 722 feet and like his tower quite unprecedented at this time.

Once the highest structure in the world, the Tower, made possible by the new material of steel with its ability to endure stresses that cast iron would not have tolerated, is now acknowledged to be somewhat ponderously designed as a piece of engineering, but it is quite masterly in its architectural exploration of spatial experience through its space-frame system of gravity-defying diagonals. It also achieves the difficult feat of making a powerful accent in the Paris scene without attempting to domineer over its great traditional monuments.

In addition to these fine works in cast iron and steel, French engineers pioneered the development of ferro, i.e. reinforced, concrete construction in the later nineteenth century, but as these innovations came to fruition architecturally mainly in the first part of the twentieth century, consideration of this aspect of their work is postponed until the next chapter.

Despite these remarkable essays in engineering architecture, 'functional' and otherwise, employing new materials and a greater skill in arranging internal dispositions than architects of the period are commonly credited with – witness Paul Sédille's *Printemps* store (1881), in which, following the Paris Opéra, he adopted for the first time the great hall rising the full height of the building (since rebuilt to an excellent but totally new design) – France at the end of the nineteenth century was still largely in the tenacious grip of the academic tradition.

This accounts for the conventional arrangement of the hôtel in the rue du Cherche-Midi, Paris, with its central entrance, cour d'honneur, and typically French treatment of windows and façade with iron balconies, and for the larger and grander neo-Baroque Petit Palais art gallery (1897) by Charles Girault, one of the most

o

PETIT PALAIS, PARIS

successful exponents of the scholarly eclecticism favoured in the second half of the century.

Well-planned, the Petit Palais has a main front which is a grandiose, balanced composition of great recessed central arched entrance portal emphasized by a drumless dome, set back and above it, with elegantly designed façades adorned with well-spaced Ionic orders – originally treated – and lavish sculpture, reaching out on either side to pedimented and domed end pavilions.

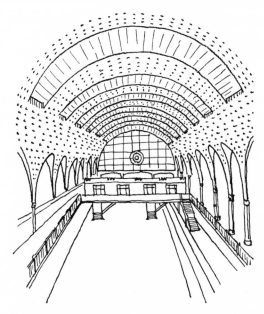

GARE D'ORSAY, PARIS

The Grand Palais (Deglane and Louvet, 1898) was also a colonnaded stone-built eclectic composition somewhat reminiscent of Garnier; though part of it was a boldly designed construction of iron and glass with crude Art Nouveau detail, still in use today. The Hôtel des Postes, Paris (1880), is the work of Julien Guadet, a typical successful architect of his time, product of the École des Beaux-Arts, winner of the Prix de Rome and member of the Academy in Rome. He also enlarged the Théâtre Français (1900) and did much domestic building. A little later the best traditional architect was V. Laloux, designer of the Gare d'Orsay (1898). Of the many educational buildings that went up in the last quarter of the nineteenth century among the most prominent are the Lycée Buffon (1889) by Vaudremer and Nénot's new Sorbonne (1900). Anstruc's Notre-Dame-du-Travail (1899) is a severe 'iron' structure more like a market hall, however, than a church.

Turning to the provinces, a notable major work of this period is the Palais des Beaux-Arts, Lille (1892), one of the thirteen regional branches of the École in Paris, by Bérard and Delmas, again owing much to tradition. Its plan shows a recessed centre and projecting wings and façades designed with a rusticated ground storey (arcaded), above which rise Corinthian columns carrying triangular and curved pediments. Above centre and wings are the steeply pitched roofs à la française.

The cathedral at Lille is a High Gothic design deriving from the work of two English experts in neo-Gothic, Henry Clutton and the better-known William Burges, though the work was altered in execution by others.

A little earlier is Charles Jacquemin Belisle's large Palais de Justice, Tours (1850), a somewhat monumental and severe essay in the classical tradition with its Roman Doric portico finished with straight entablature.

PALAIS DE JUSTICE, TOURS

Perhaps less outstanding than these examples are most of the large numbers of provincial public buildings that date from this time, many either 'Beaux Arts' or in some form of French Renaissance revival, though some are medieval. The duller efforts of the classicists constitute the *pompier* architecture of the period. For hôtels de ville a number of towns acquired older church properties, as at Rouen (the Abbey of Saint-Ouen) and Bordeaux (the Archbishop's palace).

The attempt to break the stranglehold of all this historicism, which we discern in Art Nouveau, began in the last decade of the nineteenth century, but, since the years round 1900 were a turning point in both French and in modern European architecture, a consideration of this original decorative style makes a good starting point for the next chapter.

CHAPTER NINE

The Twentieth Century

WE have already alluded to the conservatism of the French academic tradition and the École des Beaux-Arts. Because of the strength of its grip, architecture in France in the first half of the twentieth century perpetuated what were largely nineteenth-century concepts of style without improving upon the productions to which they gave birth. For this reason this chapter deliberately seeks out the most creative developments of the twentieth century in an attempt to present a meaningful pattern of architectural endeavour of significance to the present day, rather than panorama of dull and backward-looking buildings that were mostly some kind of *pastiche*.

But if the nineteenth century was mainly one of historical revivalism it also witnessed challenges being made to this traditional, stylistic conception of architecture. In new materials there were iron, steel, and glass, the early use of which has already been discussed; and there was concrete, shortly to be considered. But in the years before and after 1900 there was the phenomenon of *Art Nouveau* – the 'style moderne', as it was also referred to in France – which was an enterprising and revolutionary effort, despite its *fin de siècle* qualities, towards creating an original unhistoric style.

More a decorative than an architectural mode, with its organic, fluid, linear character Art Nouveau eventually reached France after being developed in centres as diverse as Vienna and Glasgow, Brussels and Barcelona, and its effects may be studied in the flats in the rue de la Fontaine known as the Castel Béranger (1894) in the Paris suburb of Passy, by Hector Guimard – the best of the French Art Nouveau architects, influenced by the Belgian, Horta – and in the façade of Lavirotte's Ceramic-Hôtel in the avenue de Wagram. The style was used architecturally by Binet to create a monumental gateway for the Paris exposition of 1900; but as has been said, Art Nouveau was essentially a decorative style, and as such it is best seen in the fine early twentieth-century

décor – metal, glass, faience – of Frantz Jourdain's large department store, the Samaritaine (1905), otherwise an architecturally
undistinguished building, and in the Magasin Réunis. Entrances
to the new Métro show the characteristic curvilinear manner of
Art Nouveau, e.g. the iron and glass entrance in the Place Bastille
(1900), by Guimard again, iron used externally being one of the
style's characteristics. The large steel-framed Humbert de Romans
building in Paris (1902), is also a work of this architect. Maxim's
restaurant, too, has its original Art Nouveau décor.

This is, of course, all Parisian work, but Nancy has examples to
show also, for two of the French contributors to Art Nouveau –
Émile Galle and Majorelle – hailed from that city, which had a
notable *école* with Victor Prouvé, the painter. Since the 1950's we
have seen modern architecture, after perhaps an excessive dose of
rationalism, imbued with at least something of the Art Nouveau
spirit as well as that of later Expressionism; but for the time
being, despite the strong appeal of its 'protest' element to the
anti-historicist, it proved to be a dead end, and it was to be the new
technology rather than the new motifs that was to bring on the
greatest innovations. These added up to a radically new type of
architecture that required a reconsideration of first principles,
that rejected the building as a monument, to be viewed primarily
from the outside, in favour of the manipulation of interior spaces
in the interest of function, letting the exterior express that internal
organization in a manner which was frank and logical.

Concrete, though an ancient material widely used in Roman
times, had made great strides in the nineteenth century in utilitarian structures. Joseph Monier, a gardener, invented the
principle of reinforced or ferro-concrete in the mid-nineteenth
century to counteract its weakness in tension. This allowed its
use as a beam as well as a column, and its use in architecture was
developed in the nineties by Coignet, Hennebique and Anatole
de Baudot. In spite of the resistance offered by ingrained academicism, so much part of the French Establishment, the credit for
producing buildings which were properly designed to suit the
nature of this new medium, no longer considered as a purely
functional material, must go to France.

In 1894 de Baudot, an associate of Viollet-le-Duc and therefore
an admirer of Gothic logicality, built in Saint-Jean-de-Mont-
martre the first church in reinforced concrete. It has an original
structure of great concrete arches and is roofed with a series of

domes. The sinuous decoration is of its time (1900) and effective use is made of coloured glass, as in so many French churches. It is not yet free of Gothic traditionalism, however; and Baudet did not in fact intend it to be, for the bare 'skeletal' effect was a direct allusion to the Gothic system. Looking at it with hindsight, however, we can also see modern elements which include both uncompromising frankness and spatial complication.

Apart from these suggestions towards a concrete style of the future, Le Corbusier's use of the material was first anticipated in the early works of Auguste Perret, whose block of flats 25b rue Franklin, Paris (1903), with its revolutionary placing of the 'light well' at the front and Art Nouveau ceramic tile decoration was the first ever use of reinforced concrete frame construction. With Perret's Garage Ponthieu (1905), with its hints of classicism despite the 'rose window' it boldly acknowledges the character of the new material. Their rectilinear type of design is far from the free use of curves in the contemporaneous Art Nouveau; and the garage in particular reveals the appearance of the new material too, for here the concrete is not sheathed but frankly exposed.

Perret's Théâtre des Champs-Élysées (1911) is the first public building designed with a reinforced concrete frame – based on groups of 80-foot columns – clearly displayed, though the exterior is faced with marble. Its internal arrangements, an opera auditorium, theatre hall, and intimate theatre one above the other, are also original, and so was its simplicity of style at the date it was built. Its simplicity is of a classical rather than of a functional

GARAGE PONTHIEU

variety, and there is some applied relief decoration, though the foyer is somewhat severe. Its candid 'skeletal' exposure of the structural members and the bold cantilevering of the curving auditorium balconies were portents of much that was to follow in the twentieth century. In these buildings, then, we have the earliest use of concrete architecturally, sometimes unadorned, rather than for its purely engineering properties.

Though one of the early pioneers of modern architecture, Perret had few followers in his own country because of its strong conservative tradition until the thirties when, with the increasing use of ferro-concrete as a material, architects began to turn to him for an example they could not find in the École des Beaux-Arts. From then on the revolutionary mode began to harden into a new concrete academicism, which was what in a sense Perret had intended to create.

Tony Garnier, however, the city architect of Lyon, who designed a remarkable cattle market and abattoir there in 1909 and an Olympic Stadium which achieved a steel span of 262 feet, in 1916, also made an important contribution to the development of the use of concrete in his influential design for a Cité Industrielle conceived about 1900, but not published until 1917 and little known until after the First World War when he drew upon it for his telephone exchange of 1927 and his housing development, 'Les États Unis' (1928). His contribution to the vocabulary of form of concrete architecture and his early use of the flat roof, free plan, strip windows, pilotis and open spiral staircases give him a significant niche in the history of modern architecture. He was also one of the first to consider the problems of servicing a modern building and investigated various technical possibilities in this area of design.

Here Beaux-Arts symmetry and monumentality go by the board, and concrete buildings are given plain cubic forms and adopt the cantilever principle, features soon to become hall-marks of the new architecture. But more than this, Garnier's scheme was the first real attempt to grapple with the difficulties posed by a modern city with all its problems of location and circulation. Separation of motor traffic, pedestrian precincts, functional zoning, and a community centre are all to be found in this early plan; though they are commonly thought of as recently conceived features of contemporary planning.

Some of the ideas were later implemented at Lille, and it was the starting point of Le Corbusier's equally prophetic grid-type plan for a city of three million inhabitants, the Ville Contemporaine (1922), a much more ambitious and spatially effective essay in coping with the complexities of an urban community and its zoning and traffic problems. Its ideas have since been taken up by American planners, utopian city as it was.

As we have seen, Perret was the originator of concrete architecture in the modern sense in the first decade of the twentieth century; but France, unlike Austria, Germany and Holland, did not at first take up the modern movement generally until after the First World War, when a sort of abstract classicism was the principal style in vogue.

In Perret this is combined with a superb structural rationalism that may be traced back *via* Viollet-le-Duc to the eighteenth century; and its outward characteristics are the removal of all classical detail and decoration, leaving only its satisfying proportions and its monumentality. This can be seen in Perret's masterly concrete design for the church at Le Raincy, near Paris (1922) – albeit the tower of grouped concrete columns is somewhat Expressionist – but especially in his building for the French Navy, the 'technical building' (1929) in the boulevard Victor, Paris, where the ghosts of applied orders, major and subsiding, still linger on the façades; and in the Musée des Travaux Publics, Paris, of seven years later, where, besides the concrete 'colonnades', there is a splendid curved flying staircase executed in concrete also.

As an engineer by training, however, Perret always preferred to keep to frame-and-panel forms, usually forcibly expressed in the design of his somewhat rigid reticulated façades; though he had built the first cantilevered structures in Europe and always professed a belief in the liberating effect the use of concrete would eventually have on architectural form. In this, time has proved him to be correct. As his experience of working in his chosen medium grew he refined it considerably, introducing colour and texture by the use of different aggregates into his poured and pre-cast elements and obtaining fine, sharp edges to the members.

In view of his very important and remarkable early work Perret's later career was a little disappointing in that after the Second World War, after all his advances in concrete technology, he was still working in the same essentially neo-classic mode in the blocks of flats and offices he designed at Le Havre, rebuilt

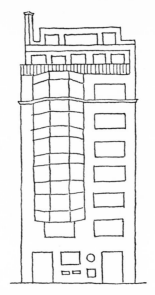

APARTMENT BLOCK, RUE GUYNEMER, PARIS

after the bombing, e.g. the Place de l'Hôtel de Ville. His work here is very traditional in its formal symmetry, but this coupled with the strict rectilinear elevations make it rather inhuman, or at any rate banal.

The blocks lack the elegance of the flats built in Paris by Michel Roux-Spitz from 1925 onwards, such as the geometrical example in the rue Guynemer; though Perret's earlier block in the rue Raynouard (1932), characteristically a frame-and-panel structure, with fine spiral staircase to his atelier, is a good example of his best work in this field and much better than his own later work at Le Havre.

On the other hand, Perret's villas and industrial buildings generally show both precision and elegance, once he is free of the need to be 'monumental' in the old way, and a noble dignity emerges from their lucid structure and excellent classic proportions.

Among his other buildings are the Esders tailoring factory (1919); the bank for the Crédit National Hôtelier (1925); the engineering works for Marioni, Montataire (1927); the panelled National Furniture Store (1929), the National School of Music, (1939) both in Paris, and from 1947 the atomic research station

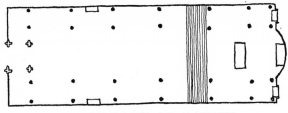

NOTRE-DAME, LE RAINCY

at Saclay; Marignane Airport; and the less successful 'skyscraper' at Amiens.

Between the wars a fair number of churches were built in France, especially in the north where they replaced those destroyed in the devastated areas; but some were to serve the new suburbs of the big cities. The earliest and most original of these churches is undoubtedly that already referred to, Notre-Dame at Le Raincy (1922), east of Paris, by Perret and his brother.

This is a traditionally planned single hall-church design, limited by a small budget which the architects turned to advantage in their bold, frank use of their favourite material, reinforced concrete, in fresh forms: slender columns, shallow, segmental

NOTRE-DAME, LE RAINCY

'barrel' vaults, and glazed openwork walls (*claustra*), achieving lightness of effect that suggests a twentieth-century re-interpretation of the spirit of the Sainte-Chapelle without any imitative historicism.

Perret's church of Saint-Joseph at Le Havre (1959), his last work, is much less successful, an extraordinary high monument like a rocket on its launching pad with hard, reticulated surfaces; though the interior structure is impressive, as one would expect from a master of reinforced concrete as Perret undoubtedly was.

But to return to the happier work, small but original, Le Raincy stands at the beginning of modern French ecclesiastical architecture and has proved to be internationally influential. The Perrets' own later Sainte-Thérèse, Montmagny (1925), owes something to it. Concrete was much used for churches from now on, though sometimes it was brick-faced under the influence of contemporary architecture in Holland, as in Besnard's Saint-Cristophe, Javel (1926); and central planning was much favoured, as in Chiral's Sainte-Jeanne-d'Arc, Charleville, and Droz and Marrat's Saint-Louis, Vincennes (1924), a spacious Greek cross design. Droz did Sainte-Jeanne-d'Arc, Nice, with its large parabolic dome, and the church of Saint-Esprit, Paris (1930), is another fine domed basilica with notable modern frescoes.

Churches built for the new suburbs of the 1930's show the economy of their budgets capitalized, as at Le Raincy. They include Azéma's Saint-Antoine-de-Padoue, Paris, and a neighbouring but very different pair, the first traditional, the second more forward-looking: P. Paquet's Church of the Cité Universitaire, Gentilly, and E. Bagge's church at Montrouge.

In spite of its extremely high academic standards French education is not noted for its readiness to adopt new methods, and in educational architecture the story has been much the same. Exceptional schools, however, have been the École Maternelle (1911) by Louis Bonnier and the infant school in the boulevard Brune, Paris, from the twenties, where the brick exterior and functional simplicity owe something to the style of the Dutchman, W. M. Dudok.

Undoubtedly the most famous pre-war French school is that at Villejuif, Paris (1932) by André Lurçat, one of the most progressive designers of the new generation which was establishing modern architecture in France. Planning emerges from a study of function, and the long main block, constructed of reinforced concrete with horizontal fenestration, is raised on slender supports to create a sheltered play area below.

School building was among the first to accept the new forms and ideas of modern architecture, but Lurçat also contributed to the evolution of domestic architecture in France, and his houses at the Cité Seurat, Paris, from the twenties and thirties were as much imitated as Le Corbusier's better known ones. Less imaginative, Lurçat was often more practical in his designs, e.g. the Villa Hefferlin, Ville-d'Avray (1931).

But before turning to the work of Le Corbusier, that figure of genius who, with a handful of other men, has dominated twentieth-century architecture so far, it is worth remarking some of the other work carried out in France during the inter-war period by the talented spirits of the time.

Thus, carrying on the tradition of the engineers of the nineteenth century, Eugène Freyssinet designed a magnificent airship hanger at Orly (1916), now destroyed, achieving a new magnitude with a span of 320 feet with a parabolic vault strengthened by ribbing, which inaugurated the principle of the 'folded slab' much developed later, especially by P. L. Nervi in Italy, the greatest contemporary concrete engineer.

But their importance does not lie solely in their structural achievement. In addition to this are their dramatic formal qualities, not superadded but emerging from the solution of the structural problems posed by this new type of concrete building. Already Freyssinet had built reinforced concrete bridges before the First World War. Like those of the Swiss engineer, Maillart, they were revolutionary in that they were conceived as monolithic structures – gone was the old division between loading and bearing – yet they were elegant and harmonious in design like good functional architecture. His road and rail bridge over the Elorn estuary in Brittany dates from 1926.

Between the wars Freyssinet experimented – mostly in industrial building – with concrete shell vaults, and developed the techniques of pre-stressing which resulted in new attenuated concrete

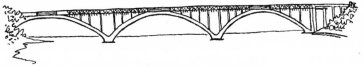

ELORN BRIDGE, BRITTANY

shapes. This can be seen in his bridges over the Marne and eventually made possible his work at Lourdes in 1958 where he engineered the vast pre-stressed concrete ribbed structure of the underground basilica. This is oval in plan with a central altar. Being as wide as possible for its height, it accommodates 22,000 pilgrims without detracting from the church and grotto.

Freyssinet had perfected a system of pre-stressing concrete, a technique which has since become so important in concrete technology; while Perret himself is also notable as one of the first architects to investigate the possibilities of standardization of building components in the light of industrial processes and the modern demand for cheaper and quicker building using good design. From the 1920's Jean Prouvé has been engaged upon the development of light, demountable, industrialized components in metal and has used them with success.

His prefabricated schools and houses, e.g. Meudon (1949), are the fruits of long study. They are very economical, as a result of their ingenious standardization, yet have an elegance and precision more usually associated with bespoke architecture, qualities which are apparent in his airy, glass-walled refreshment pavilion at Évian on Lake Geneva.

Thus his contribution is not limited to techniques and the adoption of industrialized systems. He was employing curtain-walling in the thirties as at the Maison du Peuple, Clichy (1937), where he worked with Beaudouin and Lods, but has succeeded

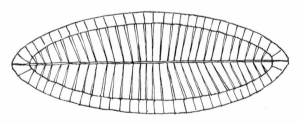

ST PIUS X BASILICA, LOURDES

in evolving new variations of what can only too often become a dull stereotype. This may be seen in the headquarters of the Building Industry Association, Paris (1950), the Technical College, Lyon, and the research institute at the University of Grenoble (1959). Prouvé has a remarkable sense of dynamic structure and organic design and because of his ability to create art out of science and mass production he is an architect-engineer whose work has much to say to designers in the second half of the twentieth century.

In 1933 Bernard Laffaille constructed the first hyperbolic paraboloid in France – that form which has begun to challenge the supremacy of the straight line in modern architecture.

Among the works of the thirties which must receive a mention are an early courageous experiment in the glazed walling of a cantilevered frame structure in the Decré Stores, Nantes (1931), Roux-Spitz's reinforced concrete book store for the Bibliothèque Nationale, Versailles (1932), the medical school at Lyon, and from 1934 the Walter Beaujon hospital, Clichy, a multi-storey block – an effective arrangement for servicing the wards – which contrasts with the very dispersed planning of the single storey 'garden' hospital at Boucicaut dating from the end of the nineteenth century; but not as advanced as the Franco-American Saint-Lô Hospital, Normandy (1956), one of the best-planned general hospitals in the world with carefully zoned subdivisions and ovoid operating theatres, providing all-round illumination. The even more recent medical school and large general hospital at Marseille by René Eggers also show how far this type of building has developed over a quarter of a century.

There are also Le Bourget airport (1937) and the hôtel de ville and high blocks of flats at Villeurbanne, a new industrial suburb of Lyon. Growing suburbs in that city and in Paris and the increasing complexity of municipal administration created a new demand for town halls, often in association with courts, police stations, libraries, etc., and one of the best of them is that of Boulogne-Billancourt (1931) by Tony Garnier and Debat-Ponsan, a rigidly formal design with large reinforced concrete frame and glazed walls.

The first exhibition after the Great War was that of the Decorative Arts (1925), which, apart from the emphasis it placed on a continuation of the pre-war decorative style, also served to advertise the reinforced concrete work of Perret, Tony Garnier and Mallet-Stevens, the Belgian; while Le Corbusier advocated 'purism' and the actual rejection of ornament in his Esprit Nouveau pavilion.

Mallet-Stevens built a number of houses in the Rue Mallet-Stevens in the mid-twenties and while they were among the most modern in France at that time a comparison with those of Lurçat and Le Corbusier show that his *avant-garde* talent was inferior to theirs. His is an exaggerated 'cubism'.

The 1937 exhibition left behind as permanent buildings the Palais de Chaillot (the New Trocadéro) and the Musée de l'Art Moderne, a somewhat controversial legacy of an otherwise well-planned exhibition. Very much of their period, they represent a sort of modernist classicism.

In our account of twentieth-century French architecture so far, Auguste Perret has emerged as the dominant figure, founder of a new 'academicism'; but the spokesman of the very small group of younger architects, who, with their rationalist version of 'neo-classicism', were laying the foundations of modern French architecture in the years immediately after the First World War, was not Perret but a pupil of his, a brilliant young Swiss of French descent who settled in Paris in 1917, Charles-Édouard Jeanneret, better known by his pseudonym of Le Corbusier.

But though Le Corbusier made his home in France he has also travelled widely, and besides working under Perret, from whom he learned about reinforced concrete design and how this could be developed from frame construction to a more organic, monolithic

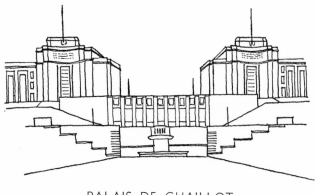

PALAIS DE CHAILLOT

type of conception (he admired Freyssinet but did not wish to adopt his forms or techniques), he also worked for Hoffmann in 1916 when he was running the Werkstätte in Vienna and served for a time in the office of Peter Behrens in Berlin, that nursery of the giants of the heroic age of modern architecture.

Through these men and his contact with the Deutscher Werkbund he became acquainted not only with the most advanced architectural ideas at that time but also with the problems of mass production techniques of industry as they applied to architecture and design, among other things hoping, unattainably at the time, for a radical mass-produced house – la maison Citrohan (1921) as he called it – that would suit the new age.

Based on constructional studies going back to 1914, there was more than one version with what were to become familiar features: two-storey living rooms, window-walls, terraces on the flat roof, and the raising of the whole 'box' clear of the ground on pilotis. The ferro-concrete construction owed a good deal to Garnier and Perret. The smooth, geometrical façades with their windows flush with the surface, have affinities both with the work of the Austrian pioneer, Adolf Loos, and with cubist painting. Above all, Le Corbusier aimed at an architecture that would match the incomparable technology of the twentieth century yet still remain humane.

Despite Le Corbusier's occasional aberrations, his inventive, exploring genius was unquestionable, and he did as much to propagate certain ideas that are now an integral part of the general philosophy of modern architecture and town planning through his writings (notably *Vers une architecture*, 1923, and *Urbanisme*, 1924), his fertile drawings and plans, and his contribution to the Congrès Internationaux d'Architecture Moderne from 1928 (notably through the Athens Charter of 1933 and his ideas of the 'functional city'), as through his actual buildings themselves. Notwithstanding this and the fact that he was an international figure, with important buildings to his credit in several continents who has deeply influenced modern architecture in Brazil, Japan, and India, some of Le Corbusier's most successful and significant work was carried out in France.

As we have seen, such was the strength of academic conservatism that little modern architecture was built in France until after the Second World War, except for some low-cost housing where its functional economy had a certain utilitarian appeal. From

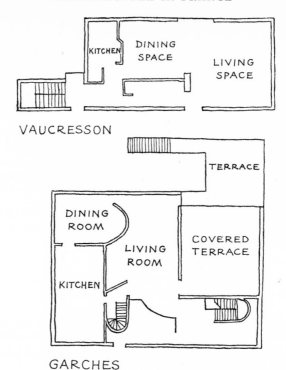

VAUCRESSON

GARCHES

LE CORBUSIER VILLAS: FIRST-FLOOR PLANS

1922–6 Le Corbusier was engaged on the Pessac housing development at Bordeaux, but there are his important 'white architecture'
villas for wealthy avant-garde clients of the late twenties, the
Maison Stein at Garches and the Villa Savoye at Poissy near
Paris.

These are built on a free plan, with walls independent of
structure, in basic geometrical shapes: rectangles, planes, cubes,
cylinders, with strip fenestration and ramps. Their affinities with
pre-war *cubisme* are obvious; Le Corbusier was himself a painter
also. But there is also an austere imaginative element present which
prevents them from becoming pure geometry, e.g. the use of
different colours on different walls and the introduction of curves
in the Villa Savoye. They make full use of the liberating effects
of modern constructional techniques. Thus internally there is a
free and functional use of space in the ingenious and complicated

VILLA SAVOYE, POISSY

planning, and they are lightly poised on pilotis or stilts and have flat roof-gardens, so that there is a tendency to allow nature to counteract the rationalism and synthetic materials which oppose it. Whatever the slogan says these houses are more than mere 'machines for living in', however much Le Corbusier might have admired grain elevators and machinery and advocate Functionalism in his writings. The latter, however, were of great value in clearing the ground for a re-examination of the premises of architecture which was part of the new philosophy. His villas Cook, Ozenfant, La Roche, and Jeanneret, all in Paris, are famous private houses of this period, and show how much modern architecture in France between the wars was very largely a matter of private patronage. Though it was contrary to the principle of 'truth to materials', they were often rendered over to produce the smooth, pure, homogeneous surface so admired by modernists at that time.

Le Corbusier's first masterpiece was the Pavillon Suisse (1932), a hostel for Swiss students in the Cité Universitaire, Paris, and in it may be detected all the main influences which had operated on him up to that time, besides his own original contribution to what has proved to be a seminal design.

Essentially it consists of a slab block related to a freer staircase block. Construction is in reinforced concrete to first-floor level, and above that is a steel frame cantilevered out and clad with factory-made components: precast concrete slabs and glass. Unlike Perret, Le Corbusier does not make prominent use of the rectilinear framework in the design of his façade and once again employs pilotis to raise the building off the floor, giving it a remarkable feeling of lightness and allowing space to flow freely underneath.

Innovations pointing to the romantic side of Le Corbusier's genius are the original use of curved stone wall to counterpoint

PAVILLON SUISSE, CITÉ UNIVERSITAIRE, PARIS

the cubist angularity, and the use of random rubble in formal and textural contrast to straight severity and smooth surfaces, features much taken up in subsequent modern architecture to become routine effects. Once more the 'organic' and the natural mitigate pure rationalism and there is a new formal freedom. Despite the novelty, however, there is still a rational separation of the functions in the volumes of the building that is both traditional and French.

The nearby Brazilian Pavilion which Le Corbusier did in 1959 with Lucio Costa – dormitory over a communal ground floor – offers a very interesting contrast, heavier and richer than its elegant predecessor.

Another work of the early thirties is the Salvation Army Hostel in Paris (the brises-soleils are a post-war embellishment), and stone rather than white stucco was used in the villa at Les Mathes (1935).

Le Corbusier has always been very much an individualist in his ideas and practice, and while these have been excessively fruitful he was incapable of creating a style that could be followed by the many, such as Walter Gropius and Ludwig Mies van der Roe evolved in Germany and Austria and later in the United States.

One of the great buildings of the mid-twentieth century, in line of descent from the Pavillon Suisse, is the heroically-conceived Unité d'Habitation, constructed at Marseille in 1952 to house 1,600 people in a single block of reinforced concrete cellular structure raised on a double row of huge stumpy tapered pilotis carrying massive beams and rising to seventeen storeys. There are twenty-three types of flat – 337 apartments in all – with two-storey living rooms (and loggias) first introduced by Le Corbusier in his Citrohan designs and the Esprit Nouveau Pavilion (1925), and subsequently developed in his flats of the 1930's.

Planning is flexible and ingenious. The section allows not only the two-storey living rooms but also the 'skip-stop' elevator, so that interior corridors are introduced only on every third floor. There is a shopping 'street' half-way up with restaurant, laundry, and post office, a nursery school on one floor and what amounts to a 'piazza' with community centre on the roof. Service machinery is placed underneath the building, but various service features (ventilators, lift-motor houses) at roof level are successfully disguised by a variety of abstract sculptural forms, notably that of the exhaust funnel.

The façades, which cleverly reduce the great scale of the sixteen-storey building by expressing what are in fact two floor levels as one, are distinguished by their 'harmonic mathematics';

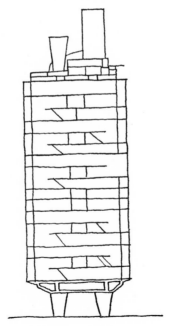

UNITÉ D'HABITATION, MARSEILLE

windows are well-shaded, being deeply recessed in the conrete frame, and primary colours are used on the balconies in contrast to the naked concrete, which is not smooth but roughly finished with the marks of the carefully-patterned shuttering apparent. Here is in 'béton brut' one of the elements of the Brutalism which has since become fashionable in architecture. The views from Unité are magnificent.

From now on in Le Corbusier's work there is an increasing sense of overall sculptural unity transcending the individual elements of which the building is composed and the contrasting sequences into which they are arranged. Characteristic is the manner in which he is able to endow with personal feeling what might so easily have become a huge impersonal cellular composition based on abstract ratios and proportions.

To appreciate the significance of the Unité d'Habitation – there were to have been six similar multiple dwellings or superblocks – one should go back to Le Corbusier's 'Ville Contemporaine', the town planning project of 1922, mentioned earlier, and the 'Ville Radieuse' (1935), where he illustrated his ideas for vertical living to escape from narrow corridor-like streets and crowding at ground level. Here to achieve this he put groups of self-contained slab blocks in a very spacious landscaped park intersected by a rectangular system of multi-level roads; but his buildings were intentionally contrasted with their environment and not intended to merge with it organically. Le Corbusier was very much concerned with what constituted an ideal human environment, and his work as an architect should not really be separated from his ideas as a planner. This approach of his is becoming more and more typical of that of the modern architect, who, unlike his nineteenth-century predecessor, thinks in terms of total environment much more than of isolated buildings and tends increasingly to contribute as one of a synoptic team. What the long-term effects of this will be on architecture as an art in the traditional sense, as something more than social technology, only time will tell.

The Unité d'Habitation at Nantes-Rezé (1955), Le Corbusier's second 'maison radieuse', is rather less successful than the first, heavier, despite the more slender piers and simpler roof; and it abandons the double-height living room. But it is still a strong design and like Le Corbusier's work at Briey-la-Forêt (1960) reveals another facet of his imagination.

Carefully proportioned on his famous Modulor system, a series of related dimensions based on the proportions of an ideal human figure, with which (despite its somewhat odd application to buildings of prefabricated units) Le Corbusier's architecture is given a new classicism adapted to contemporary conditions but traditionally French in its logic, these great structures are an excellent solution to the problem of mass housing in the twentieth century, combining individual privacy for families with the enjoyment of spacious settings and communal services.

The most outstanding examples of recent religious architecture have also come from the fertile genius of Le Corbusier, both of them later works in the canon. His capacity to produce the inimitable is demonstrated by the small but justly celebrated hill-top pilgrimage chapel, Notre-Dame-du-Haut, at Ronchamp (1950), some miles west of Belfort, where concrete is no longer used in the logical, classical 'post and lintel' manner of Perret but moulded monolithically into curious apparently arbitrary abstract sculptural forms. This is something of a volte-face from his 'cubist-functional' architecture of the twenties; this is no 'machine for praying in' but a masterly antithesis of rational architecture.

There is a carefully contrived strangeness about its white façade battered inwards with window openings of all sizes and shapes seemingly disposed at random, and the bow-like angle at which the main walls meet. Unlike much modern architecture, solids very much dominate voids here, and there is irrationality in the

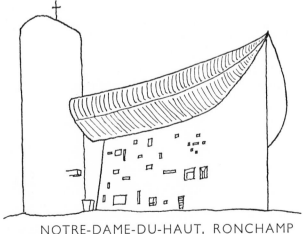

NOTRE-DAME-DU-HAUT, RONCHAMP

curved and billowy shell-like projecting roof in brown concrete and in the tall cylindrical chapel. The interior is wonderfully sculptural and plastic, strangely lit by coloured glass from windows with very deep reveals, patches of light contrasting with the shadowy areas in a highly dramatic and emotional way.

Significantly, perhaps, this new development of plastic form in Le Corbusier's work came after his visit to Brazil and his experience there of Oscar Niemeyer's concrete structures. It is a poetic protest against the excessive cerebration of the rationalists and as such an important monument, a long way from functionalism – except that many have found Ronchamp evokes a profoundly religious mood. Yet 'functionalism' in the material rather than spiritual sense, as a universal discipline in modern architecture, is still valid, and the influence of such works as Ronchamp and the revival of neo-expressionism and the cult of architectural personality will not be beneficial if in the long run they lead to a narrow 'form for form's sake' rather than to an enrichment of the general philosophy and vocabulary of modern architecture.

An unusual commission for a contemporary architect is that for the Dominican noviciate monastery Le Couvent Sainte-Marie-de-la-Tourette (1957) at Éveux, some sixteen miles north-west of Lyon, where Le Corbusier used raw concrete to make strong, brutally direct statements and produced a remarkable design of considerable monumentality, where square-cut shapes and a modular system replace the sculptural effects of Ronchamp.

The monastery, which is stepped down a steeply sloping hillside, consists of a **U**-shaped arrangement of conventual blocks round a central courtyard with a tall, narrow, mysteriously withdrawn chapel, without direct lighting, at the open end. The massive

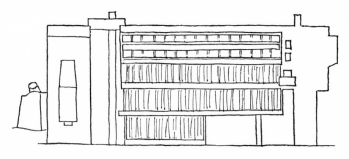

MONASTERY OF LA TOURETTE, ÉVEUX

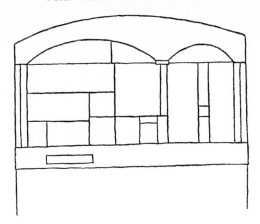

MAISONS JAOUL, NEUILLY

solidity of the latter contrasts in character and rhythm with the horizontal conventual blocks, which are relatively outward-looking – appropriate to Dominicans – with their common rooms and libraries with glazed walls below and two storeys of rugged cell accommodation cantilevered out above. At the very top runs a roof cloister and below on one side are refectory and kitchen. Despite these different elements, however, an impressive unity is attained.

Le Corbusier's Maisons Jaoul at Neuilly date from 1954 and shows the new style applied to villa architecture, with much emphasis on exposed brickwork; but it is now time to pass on from one whose influence is to be seen everywhere in architecture in the modern idiom, and whose planning ideas evolved continuously from his *Urbanism* (1925) to *Les Trois Établissements Humains* (1945), to consider French housing developments in this century other than those of the Unités.

In general, the aspect of French towns which is still dominant despite changes is that of the classical vernacular: well-bred and civilized in the true sense of the word, if sometimes rather dull. In Paris suburbs, Tergnier, and the Foyer Rémois, near Reims, the garden city ideas emanating from England in the early years of the century did have some effect, but are somewhat foreign to the native genius. At Drancy, for example, the high building is much more in keeping with the French apartment house tradition.

The French have, until recently, been slow to develop an

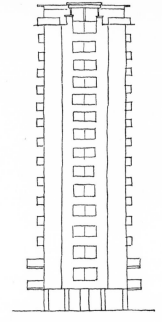

POINT BLOCK, DRANCY

adequate housing programme, perhaps inhibited by the size of the problem inherited from the devastation of the war years (the last war left two million homeless), and handicapped by an antiquated and fragmented building industry and the national tendency to place other items before the home higher up in the list of priorities.

Moreover, France has no tradition of modern town planning, the results of which may be seen in the arid rigidity of Perret's Le Havre, where no provision is made for 'neighbourhoods' or traffic circulation. Even some of the developments round Paris, such as Épinay-sur-Seine, or La Meinau, Strasbourg, show what seems an innate preference for theoretically rigid and uncompromisingly rectilinear plans; though those of Émile Aillaud's Cité de l'Abreuvoir, Paris-Bobigny and Cité des Courtilières, Paris-Pantin (1959) are commendable attempts to get away from this with their continuous serpentine blocks, cylindrical and three-point blocks, their greater variety of space and perspective, and their greater respect for the individualities of the terrain.

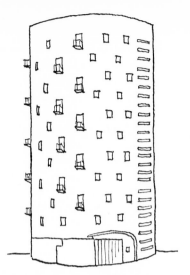

CYLINDRICAL TOWER BLOCK, BOBIGNY

Aillaud's employment of colour here shows how, sensitively and thoughtfully applied, it may be used to enhance the architectural and psychological qualities of a large design, and reminds us that of modern architects in France Le Corbusier, perhaps because he was a painter, was among the first to experiment with its possibilities, e.g. the early example of the Pessac housing near Bordeaux. The best of the recent town plans is that for Marly-les-Grandes-Terres (1958), ten miles west of Paris, by Marcel Lods and J. J. Honneger. Here, on a low plateau, a community of 6,000 is housed in nine well-spaced groups of apartment blocks enclosed in a single traffic route, to which vehicles are restricted and therefore separated from pedestrian movement.

The individual buildings, however, are still too uniform and repetitious – without lifts for five storeys – but the centre of shops and offices disposed round a large garden area is attractive, freer, and more imaginative. Schools are provided as an integral part of the plan. Hot water is distributed from a central plant and there are ample parking facilities.

'Les Buffets', the most successful part of Fontenay-aux-Roses, the Nuclear Studies Centre, also confines traffic to the periphery, while another manifestation of the new France is the industrial and associated housing development at Lacq in the Pyrenees, where the great natural gas field is being exploited. Outstanding is the Société Nationale des Pétroles d'Aquitaine's complex (1961) by de Brauer, well planned with a magnificent water tower, huge but elegant, and the civic centre and mixed development housing for 15,000 at Moureux, still with a tendency to rigidity and abstraction, however. The Strasbourg suburb of Cité Rotterdam (1952) is by Eugène Beaudouin who had collaborated with Lods on the mixed development at Drancy, back in the thirties. The latter has also done work for the French ministries of Education and War.

Other industrial and commercial buildings of note include the splendidly engineered exhibition hall of the Centre National des Industries et des Techniques (1958), at the opposite end of the Champs-Élysées from the Louvre, where Prouvé and P. L. Nervi have provided the largest concrete vaults in the world to cover the glass-walled triangle with several levels of floor space, creating a magnificent interior where vastness is not inimical to grace. Externally it is less engaging. The Saint Gobain Building by Aubert, Bonin, and Marican (1959) is the newest and largest seven-storey office block with ancillary buildings on a landscaped site. Modular construction, glass curtain walls, and flexible internal planning combine to produce a building that is at once practical and handsomely rational.

These two buildings are both in Paris. So is the UNESCO Building (1958), which is well-adapted to the eighteenth-century Place de Fontenoy. But the façades of the **Y**-shaped eight storey Secretariat by the architects Marcel Breuer (an inventor of tubular steel furniture in the twenties) and Bernard Zehrfuss are unduly cluttered with brises-soleils, a feature of modern architecture devised by Le Corbusier who has made excellent use of their aesthetic potentialities. The best part is the accomplished

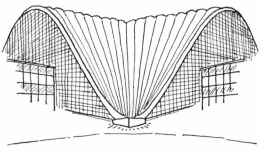

C.N.I.T. EXHIBITION HALL, PARIS

concrete structure and splendid trapezoidal conference hall by Nervi. Zehrfuss, a post-war architect, was one of the architects of the C.N.I.T. exhibition building and his industrial work include the premises of the Mame printing company at Tours and the factory at Flins (1953) for Renault cars. Current work by Breuer, only given major opportunities as an international designer in the last fifteen years, includes a mountain town project in the Haute Savoie and a large office block in Nice, raised on pilotis, with ramifying plan and 'sculptural' façade of pre-cast concrete units.

But many of the most interesting and successful modern buildings in France are churches. A particular feature is their fine use of glass as in Maurice Novarina's church at Audincourt (1950), where it is by Léger and Jean Bazaine, and in Saint-Rémy, in the glass town of Baccarat (1957), where Nicolas Kazi's exposed concrete structure is coupled with splendid effects of richly coloured glass. Exposed concrete construction is also a feature of Notre-Dame, Royan (1958), by Gillet, associate engineers Laffaile

NOTRE-DAME, ROYAN

and Sarger. Oval in plan, it has huge **V**-shaped piers opening outwards with vertical bands of glass between and an independent concrete roof high above its sunken floor – a most energetic and creative design. Royan, a much damaged coastal town, has a good deal of new development, including a variety of housing and a large circular market hall (1956), covered with undulating concrete paraboloid vaulting. It is interesting to contrast it with the concrete market at Reims (1930) by Maigrot, an early attempt at a wide span without interior supports. At the end of 1968 Les Halles, the markets of central Paris, were demolished and transferred to larger and more efficient Rungis, well-sited near Orly on the edge of the city providing the council with a solution to an old problem and affording new opportunities for redevelopment.

Until recently France has been one of the poorest housed countries in Europe: partly as a result of the economic setback induced by war, partly because of the reluctance of the French to spend on housing. Thus almost 25 per cent of all dwellings have lacked an inside water supply, while the average age of Parisian houses was ninety years. But now at last new building methods and modern architecture are beginning to catch up with French progress in industry and transportation, and a twentieth-century vernacular, of which the riverside redevelopment at Rouen is another good example, is emerging. Yet the architecture of today is also part of tomorrow's history and this aspect is not forgotten in modern France. In addition to the preservation of individual old buildings of special interest or merit it is now recognized that the conservation of entire urban areas may in some instances be necessary – the Renaissance centre of the great city of Lyon is one such example – in order to retain their special value and provide a psychologically important 'sense of identity' for the citizens of tomorrow's mass society. It is an example we would do well to follow in Britain.

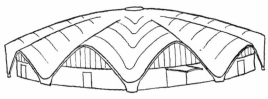

MARKET HALL, ROYAN

GLOSSARY

abacus: the flat slab on top of a capital.

acanthus: a conventionalized leaf ornament in classical decoration.

acroterion: a plinth for an ornament (or both together) set at the apex and corners of a pediment.

aedicule: the frame of a niche or opening in classical architecture consisting of two columns supporting an entablature and pediment.

aisle: lower division of a basilica or church parallel to the nave, choir, or transept from which it is divided by pillars.

ambulatory: an aisle round an apse or circular building or across the east end of a church.

amphitheatre: an oval or elliptical building with an arena surrounded by tiers of seats.

appartement: a suite of private rooms for family use.

apse: the semi-circular or polygonal end of a basilica, church, or side chapel.

aqueduct: an artificial water channel, usually elevated on a brick or stone structure.

arabesque: in classical architecture, intricate surface decoration made up of delicate flowing foliage forms with figures and other motifs, sometimes symbolic or grotesque.

arcade: a range of arches carried on columns or piers; 'blind' if attached to a wall.

architrave: the bottom member of an entablature.

archivolt: an architrave moulding following the lines of an arch.

arras: tapestry from Arras used as a wall hanging before the advent of wood panelling.

arris: a sharp edge where two surfaces meet.

ashlar: masonry of smooth squared stones set in regular courses.

astylar: of a classical façade without columns or pilasters.

attic: a low storey above a main cornice; more loosely a lower top storey or space within the roof.

baldacchino: a canopied structure (usually over an altar) supported on columns.

barbican: outwork or detached feature protecting the approach to a castle.

barrel vault: an arched stone covering running the length of a building or apartment.

base: lower part of a structure; a flat, circular, moulded slab supporting a column in a classical order.

basse-court: 'low court', i.e. the outer court of a medieval castle or, later, the service court of a château.

basilica: a Roman public hall or Early Christian church based on its plan; by extension, a medieval church with aisles and clerestory.

bastide: a small fortified medieval town laid out on a rectilinear plan. Mostly in south-west France.

bay: a vertical unit of a wall or façade; also a compartment of a nave or aisle.

bel-étage: piano nobile.

billet: Romanesque ornament consisting of short cylindrical or square blocks set alternately as a moulding.

boulevard: a wide avenue planted with trees; properly when laid out on the site of demolished ramparts.

brise-soleil: a 'sun break' of fins or baffles to shade windows in a sunny climate.

buttress: a projecting vertical mass of masonry stiffening a wall or resisting an outward thrust. **flying buttress:** an arched prop of masonry resisting the lateral pressure of a wall or vault.

cabinet: a small private room.

calidarium: the hot room of Roman thermae.

cantilever: a projecting beam or slab held down at the wall end by a superincumbent weight or in some other way.

capital: the moulded or carved block on top of a column.

cella: the central enclosed portion of a Roman temple, excluding the portico.

chancel: the eastern part of a church reserved for the clergy and choir.

channel: a groove or fluting in a plain surface or column.

château: a medieval French castle; later a large country house.

chevet: the east end of a medieval church which consists of an apse surrounded by an ambulatory and sometimes by radiating chapels.

chevron: zig-zag moulding which is often found round Romanesque openings.

choir: the portion of a church set aside for clergy and choir, divided off from the rest by a screen.

clerestory: the upper part of a wall with windows, as in the nave of a church above the aisle roof.

clocher: a French bell tower.

cloister: a covered walk in a monastery or college arranged round a square court.

coffering: panels sunk deeply into the surface of a ceiling.

colonnade: a range of columns.

colonnette: a small column.

column: a vertical member in classical architecture consisting of a base, round shaft, and capital designed to carry an entablature or arch; but also used non-structurally.

console: in classical architecture a bracket in the form of an **S**-shaped scroll.

corbel: a projecting stone bracket. **corbelling:** a series of corbels extending progressively farther forward, one above the other.

cornice: the projecting upper portion of an entablature, or any projecting top course.

corps de logis: the principal residential block of a large house, as distinct from its wings or pavilions.

cour d'honneur: the principal entrance court of a large house or château.

crenellation: battlements.

cresting: a run of repeated ornament along the top of a roof or wall; often pierced.

crocket: a curved leaf-like ornament in Gothic architecture.

cruciform: cross-shaped.

crypt: a space under a building, usually under the chancel of a church and used for burial.

cubiform: cube-shaped.

cupola: a spherical roof over a square, circular, or polygonal apartment.

cusp: a curved projection round a Gothic arch, or opening, separating 'foils'.

cyclopean: a term used loosely to describe masonry of very large polygonal blocks.

dais: a platform at the end of a hall.

domical vault: a webbed vault, over a square or polygonal apartment, resembling a dome.

donjon: the keep or main block of a castle.

dormer: a window with vertical sides projecting from a sloping roof.

echinus: a rounded projecting moulding supporting the abacus of a Doric capital.

eclectic: of a style selecting elements from a variety of sources.

enceinte: the area enclosed by castle walls or fortifications.

enfilade: a suite of rooms arranged along an axis.

entablature: the horizontal top part of a classical order consisting of architrave, frieze, and cornice.

entasis: the swelling of a classical column to correct the optical illusion of concavity.

enresol: a mezzanine.

exedra: in classical architecture a recess or alcove, semi-circular or rectangular, fitted with seating. Also applied to the niche or apse of a church.

façade: the face or front of a building.

Q

finial: ornamental top part of a spire, gable, or pinnacle.

Flamboyant: The French late Gothic style so-called from its fondness for curvilinear tracery of flame-like forms. O. Fr. *flambe*, a flame.

flèche: a spirelet, i.e. a diminutive wooden spire.

fleur-de-lis: the lily, the royal arms of France.

fluting: vertical channelling on the shaft of a column.

foliate: leaf-like.

forum: a space for assembly and market at the centre of a Roman town, surrounded by public buildings and colonnades.

french window (or door): a tall window opening in two leaves like a pair of doors.

fresco: a wall painting; properly one executed 'fresh' on wet plaster.

frieze: the middle member of an entablature or, in a room, the space between the top of the panelling and the cornice or ceiling.

frigidarium: the cooling room of Roman thermae.

gallery: the upper storey above a church aisle and opening on to the nave; also called a tribune and sometimes, erroneously, a triforium.

Greek cross: cross with all four arms of equal length.

groin: an edge formed by intersecting vaults; an arris.

groin vault: a cross vault produced by the intersection of two tunnel vaults.

hôtel particulier : a large French town house.

hôtel de ville: a French town hall.

Hôtel-Dieu: 'House of God', i.e. a large town hospital of religious foundation.

hypocaust: a chamber below ground level heated by hot air from the furnace; the Roman system of heating a building or important room.

impost: a course or moulding from which an arch springs.

intercolumniation: the distance between two classical columns measured in diameters.

Latin cross: a cross with one of the four arms elongated.

lierne: a decorative rib in a Gothic vault which does not spring from the wall or touch the central boss.

lintel: a horizontal member spanning an opening.

loggia: a covered gallery behind an open arcade or colonnade.

louvre: ventilator in a roof or wall, usually slatted.

lunette: a semi-circular or crescent-shaped opening or surface, e.g. a tympanum.

machicolations: floor openings in the stone parapet of a crenellated wall.

mansard roof: a roof of double pitch, the lower longer and steeper. (After F. Mansart but actually earlier.)

metope: a panel between triglyphs on a Doric frieze.

mezzanine: an entresol or low intermediate storey.

module: the measure of proportion by which the parts of a classical building are regulated; in modern practice a convenient unit upon which all the dimensions of a building and its components are based for economy and ease of construction.

motte: the steep mound of an eleventh- or twelfth-century castle.

mouchette: a curved dagger motif in late Gothic tracery.

mouldings: contours of projecting members.

mullion: a vertical division between the lights of a window.

narthex: a porch in front of the nave and aisles of some churches.

nave: the main division of a church west of the chancel arch or crossing, with or without aisles.

oculus: a circular opening.

œil de bœuf window: a small circular window.

ogive: French term for a pointed arch.

ogivale: the French Gothic style.

orchestra: in a classical theatre the circular space for the chorus in front of the stage.

order: in classical architecture, a column (consisting of base, shaft, and capital) with the entablature it supports, proportioned and decorated to an accepted mode. In medieval architecture, a ring of voussoirs in an arch.

orientation: the positioning of a building in relation to the points of the compass. Most churches are aligned east-west with the altar at the east end, but Early Christian churches were 'orientated' westwards.

pavillon: a pavilion, i.e. a subdivision of some larger building like a château, either almost detached or projecting at an angle or termination of a main block. Also a small light ornamental building.

pedestal: a base supporting a column, obelisk, or statue in classical architecture.

pediment: the triangular end of the moderately pitched roof of a classical building above the top of the entablature or cornice. A similar but smaller form used over doors or windows, sometimes segmental.

pendentive: a concave spandrel marking the transition between a square or polygonal apartment and a circular dome, cf. squinch arch.

peripteral: of a classical building having a surrounding row of free-standing columns.

peristyle: a continuous colonnade surrounding a classical building or court.

piano nobile: the main floor of an important residence when the principal reception rooms are above a ground floor or basement.

pier: the solid support of a pair of arches in an arcade.

pilaster: a rectangular column usually engaged with a wall but projecting from it.

pilotis: a modern French term for stilts which raise a building clear of the ground.

pinnacle: a tapering termination of a vertical form.

podium: the platform on which a building is raised or the lowest part of a pedestal.

porphyry: a red and white crystalline rock.

portail: the entrance front of a great church, not just the porch or portal.

portal: an elaborately designed, often recessed, doorway of a large building.

portcullis: a vertically sliding grid designed to obstruct a castle entrance.

porte-cochère: a porch large enough to admit a coach and so provide a covered entrance.

portico: a roofed space open at least on one side and enclosed by a range of columns supporting the roof.

postern: a concealed exit or sally port in military architecture.

pre-cast concrete: concrete cast in a factory or on site before being positioned, i.e. not poured *in situ.*

pre-stressed concrete: pre-cast, reinforced concrete artificially stressed before use, by tensioning inserted wire cables, to obtain more efficient and economic use of materials.

prostyle: having a portico of free-standing columns.

prothesis: a part of a church where the elements of the Eucharist were set out.

pseudo-peripteral: of a classical building having a surrounding row of pilasters or engaged columns only.

quatrefoil: circular or square opening having four 'foils' or leaves separated by 'cusps'. A trefoil has three foils, a cinquefoil has five.

quoins: the corner stones at the angle of a building, especially when rusticated.

reinforced concrete: ferro-concrete; concrete, the tensile strength of which has been greatly increased by embedding in it steel rods and mesh.

reredos: a decorated wall or screen behind and above the altar in a church.

retro-choir: the space at the back of the high altar in a large church.

rib: a stone arch on the groin or surface of a vault.

rose window: a circular Gothic window with tracery in a radiating pattern.

rotunda: a circular building, usually domed.

roundel: a round decorative panel.

rustication: stonework of large freestone blocks (rough or smooth) with recessed joints.

salon: a large reception room in a hôtel or château.

sanctuary: specifically the holiest part of a church, i.e. the presbytery portion of the chancel.

scroll: an ornamental motif in the form of a partly unrolled parchment.

squinch arch: a small arch across the inner angle of a compartment making the transition to a circular dome or polygonal structure above, cf. pendentive.

string course: a projecting horizontal band along a wall.

stucco: plaster applied to a wall or ceiling surface; usually moulded decoratively when used internally or smoothed and painted externally.

stylobate: the platform of a classical temple, usually of three steps.

swag: a festoon of fruit, flowers, and foliage.

tepidarium: the warm room of Roman thermae.

term: a terminal figure, or sculptured bust, to a pedestal or pillar.

terra cotta: a burnt clay material harder than brick.

tessellated: of a cement surface in which tesserae are set.

tesserae: small cubes of marble, stone, or glass used in mosaic work.

thermae: Roman public baths-cum-social centres.

tierceron: an intermediate rib in a Gothic vault between a main springer and the ridge rib.

tracery: intersecting bars of moulded stone forming patterns in Gothic windows.

transept: either arm of the transverse part of a cruciform church.

triapsidal: having three apses.

tribune: the apse of a basilica or rostrum; also the gallery of a church.

triforium: a wall passage above the arcade and open to the nave.

triglyph: a block with three vertical grooves between metopes in a Doric frieze.

tunnel vault: see barrel vault.

tympanum: in classical architecture the triangular area within the pediment and the space between the base and cornice of a pedestal. Otherwise, the area between a lintel and the arch over it.

undercroft: a vaulted basement.

urbanisme: town-planning.

vault: an arched covering of stone.

velarium: a large awning supported on masts.

venetian window: a semi-circular headed opening flanked by two narrower flat-headed ones; the Serlian motif.

vermiculation: ornament resembling worm tracks carved on masonry.

vernacular: of buildings in the native provincial idiom.

vesica (piscis): a vertically pointed oval shape in medieval art, usually containing a sacred figure. A mandorla.

vestibule: an ante-room or entrance hall.

villa: a large Roman farmstead or country house, the centre of an estate. From Renaissance times either a country house or a *villa suburbana*.

volute: the scroll of an Ionic or Corinthian capital.

voussoir: a wedge-shaped block forming part of an arch.

wheel window: see rose window.

BIBLIOGRAPHY

Adams, H. *Mont-Saint-Michel and Chartres* (Constable, 1936)

Allsopp, B. *History of Classical Architecture* (Pitman, 1963)

Allsopp, B. *History of Renaissance Architecture* (Pitman, 1959)

Aubert, M. and Goubet, S. *Gothic Cathedrals of France and their Treasures*, trans. by Kochan and Millard (Vane, 1959)

Aubert, M. and Goubet, S. *Romanesque Cathedrals and Abbeys of France*, trans. by C. Girdlestone (Vane, 1966)

Banham, R. *Theory and Design in the First Machine Age* (Architectural Press, 1960)

Bazin, G. *Baroque and Rococo* (Thames & Hudson, 1964)

Blake, P. *Le Corbusier* (Penguin, 1963)

Blomfield, R. *History of French Architecture, 1494–1774*, 4 vols. (Maclehose, 1936)

Blunt, A. *Art and Architecture in France, 1500–1700* (Pelican History of Art) (Penguin, 1956)

Boesiger, W. *Architectural Works of Le Corbusier*, 1910–1965 (Thames & Hudson, 1967)

Bony, J. and Hürlimann, M. *French Cathedrals* (Thames & Hudson, 1961)

Bowie, T. *Sketchbook of Villard de Honnecourt* (New York, 1959)

Branner, R. *Burgundian Gothic Architecture* (Zwemmer, 1960)

Branner, R. *Gothic Architecture* (Prentice-Hall, 1962)

Branner, R. *Saint Louis and the Court Style in French Architecture* (Zwemmer, 1964)

Brogan, O. *Roman Gaul* (Bell, 1953)

Butterfield, H. *A Short History of France* (C.U.P., 1959)

Choay, F. *Le Corbusier* (Mayflower, 1960)

Clapham, A. W. *Romanesque Architecture in Western Europe* (O.U.P., 1936)

Collins, P. *Changing Ideals in Modern Architecture, 1750–1950* (Faber, 1965)

Collins, P. *Concrete, the Vision of a New Architecture* (Faber, 1959)

Conant, K. J. *Carolingian and Romanesque Architecture: 800–1200* (Pelican History of Art) (Penguin, 1959)

Connolly, C. and Zerbe, J. *Les Pavillons: French Pavilions of the 18th Century* (Hamish Hamilton, 1962)

Cook, T. *Twenty Five Great Houses of France* (Rivington)

Daniel, G. *Megalith Builders of Western Europe* (Hutchinson, 1963)

Daniel, G. *Prehistoric Chamber Tombs of France* (Thames & Hudson, 1960)

Dickinson, R. *The West European City* (Routledge, 1962)

Doyon, G. and Habrecht, R. *L'architecture rurale et bourgeoise en France* (Paris, 1942).

Duby, G. and Mandrou, R. *History of French Civilisation* (Weidenfeld & Nicolson, 1966)

Duby, G. *Europe of the Cathedrals, 1140-1280* (Zwemmer, 1966)

Dutton, R. *Châteaux of France* (Batsford, 1957)

Dutton, R. *The Land of France* (Batsford, 1952)

Evans, J. *Art in Medieval France, 987-1498* (O.U.P., 1952)

Evans, J. *Monastic Architecture in France from Renaissance to Revolution* (C.U.P., 1964)

Fletcher, B. *History of Architecture*, revised by R. A. Cordingley (Athlone Press, 1961)

Focillon, H. *Art of the West in the Middle Ages*, vol. 1, Romanesque; vol. 2, Gothic, trans. by J. Boney (Phaidon, 1963)

Frankl, P. *Gothic Architecture* (Pelican History of Art) (Penguin, 1963)

Gantner, J. *Romanesque Art in France* (Thames & Hudson, 1957)

Gardner, A. *Introduction to French Church Architecture* (C.U.P., 1938)

Gebelin, F. *Châteaux of France* (Benn, 1966)

Gimpel, J. *The Cathedral Builders*, trans. by C. F. Barnes (New York, 1961)

Gloag, J. *Guide to Western Architecture* (Allen & Unwin, 1958)

Harvey, J. *The Gothic World, 1100-1160* (Batsford, 1950)

Hautecoeur, L. *Histoire de l'Architecture Classique en France*, 4 vols. (Paris, 1943-55)

Hitchcock, H. R. *Architecture: Nineteenth and Twentieth Centuries* (Pelican History of Art) (Penguin, 1963)

Hitchcock, H. R. *World Architecture* (Hamlyn, 1963)

Howarth, T. *Nineteenth and Twentieth Century Architecture* (Longmans, 1963)

Howgrave-Graham, R. *Cathedrals of France* (Batsford, 1959)

Hughes, J. and Lynton, N. *Renaissance Architecture* (Longmans, 1962)

Hürlimann, M. and Valery, P. *France* (Thames & Hudson, 1957)

Jackson, T. G. *Gothic Architecture in France, England and Italy* (C.U.P., 1915)

Jackson, T. G. *Renaissance of Roman Architecture, part III, France* (C.U.P., 1923)

Jantzen, H. *High Gothic* (Constable, 1962)

Joedicke, J. *History of Modern Architecture* (Architectural Press, 1959)

Kimball, F. *The Creation of Rococo* (Oldbourne, 1943)

Lasteyrie, R. de. *L'architecture religieuse en France à l'époque gothique*, 2 vols. (Paris, 1926)

Lavedan, P. *French Architecture* (Penguin, 1956)

Le Corbusier. *Towards a New Architecture*, trans. by F. Etchells (Architectural Press, 1947)

Le Corbusier. *My Work* (Architectural Press, 1960)

Lees-Milne, J. *Baroque Europe* (Batsford, 1962)

Levron, J. *The Royal Châteaux of the Île de France* (Allen & Unwin, 1963)

Levron, J. *Châteaux of the Loire* (Kaye, 1963)

Lowry, B. *Renaissance Architecture* (Prentice-Hall, 1962)

Mâle, E. *The Gothic Image* (Collins, 1961)

Maurois, A. *An Illustrated History of France* (Bodley Head, 1960)

Michel, F. O. and Gisler C. *A Guide to the Art Treasures of France* (Methuen, 1966).

Millon, H. A. *Baroque and Rococo Architecture* (Prentice-Hall, 1962)

Mumford, L. *The City in History* (Penguin, 1966)

Nairn, I. *Nairn's Paris* (Penguin, 1968)

Ormsby, H. *France: A Regional and Economic Geography* (Methuen, 1950)

Panofsky, E. *Abbot Suger on the Art Treasures of Saint-Denis* (Princeton, 1947)

Pevsner, N. *Outline of European Architecture* (Penguin, 1964)

Pevsner, N. *Pioneers of Modern Design* (Penguin, 1960)

Plommer, H. *Ancient and Classical Architecture* (Longmans, 1956)

Richards, J. M. *Introduction to Modern Architecture* (Penguin, 1956)

Richardson, A. E. *The Art of Architecture* (E.U.P., 1938)

Ritchie, R. L. *France: A Companion to French Studies* (Methuen, 1951)

Robertson, D. S. *Greek and Roman Architecture* (C.U.P., 1943)

Rosenau, H. *Boullée's Treatise on Architecture* (Tiranti, 1953)

Rowe, V. *Châteaux of the Loire* (Putnam, 1954)

Rowe, V. *Royal Châteaux of Paris* (Putnam, 1956)

Russell, J. *Paris* (Batsford, 1960)

Saalman, H. *Medieval Architecture: European 600–1200* (Prentice-Hall, 1962)

Scully, V. *Modern Architecture* (Prentice-Hall, 1962)

Smith, G. E. Kidder. *New Architecture of Europe* (Penguin, 1962)

Stewart, C. *Gothic Architecture* (Longmans, 1961)

Tapie, V. L. *The Age of Grandeur: Baroque and Classicism in Europe* (Weidenfeld & Nicolson, 1960)

Taraion, J. *Treasures of the Churches of France* (Thames & Hudson, 1966)

Tuulse, A. *Castles of the Western World* (Thames & Hudson, 1959)

Ward, W. H. *Architecture of the Renaissance in France, 1495–1830*, 2 vols. (Batsford, 1926)

Whittick, A. *European Architecture in the Twentieth Century*, 2 vols. (Lockwood, 1950–53)

INDEX

References to illustrations are in *italic*